W9-CBI-456

Country Ways

Secrets for Finding and Keeping a Country Man

JOYCE MARLOW

WARNER BOOKS

A Time Warner Company

Warner Books, Inc., 1271 Avenue of the Americas, New York, NY 10020
Visit our Web site at http://warnerbooks.com
A Time Warner Company

Printed in the United States of America
First Printing: February 1999
10 9 8 7 6 5 4 3 2 1

Library of Congress Cataloging-in-Publication Data

Marlow, Joyce.
Country ways : secrets for finding and keeping a country man / Joyce Marlow.
p. cm.
ISBN 0-446-52401-8
1. Mate selection—United States. 2. Rural men—United States. 3. Country life—United States.
HQ801.M3717 1999 98-7596
306.82—dc21 CIP

Book design by Giorgetta Bell McRee

For Walt,
my best friend in life and love

Acknowledgments

I couldn't have written this book without the help of some very special people I'm grateful to call friends. My daughter Heather for her terrific ideas, editing skills, and cheerleading; my sister Bonnie Tallman for laughing in all the right places; my sister-at-heart and staunchest supporter Sheila Slattery; and Walt for showing me the richness and wonder of country life.

Warmest thanks to my agent Maureen Walters and my editor Caryn Karmatz Rudy, who helped shape this book in countless ways and answered my many questions with unfailing patience and good cheer. A special note of appreciation to everyone at Warner Books for bringing *Country Ways* to city women everywhere. Country men may never be the same!

Contents

Section Two: Relationships—Country Style 65

SECTION THREE:
Adjusting to Country Life 137

Introduction

Do you dream of finding a man who'll light a fire in the fireplace (and your heart) on a chilly night? A man who's romantic, both your best friend *and* your lover? A man not just willing, but *wanting* to make a commitment? A man who dreams of finding a woman to love and cherish for the rest of his life; someone who wants what you want—to be together and to stay together?

Maybe you've been looking in all the wrong places.

Maybe it's time to consider embracing life in the "past" lane.

Country Ways is about *real* relationships based on honesty, trust, and understanding. Relationships aren't games where one person wins and the other loses. And they aren't based on being mysterious and playing hard to get. A charade may catch a man's interest, but how long can you pretend? Get real, and get a man! And while you're at it, get one worth keeping.

Country men are some of the last good men around. Caring, hardworking men with strong opinions and hearts of gold. Men who know it's tough to find a good woman and who're willing to go the distance to keep one. Intelligent, capable men who are strong enough to value an independent woman. Men who actually *like* women and if you already have kids will like them, too.

Does the idea of leaving the city for a slower, gentler life sound appealing? Do you yearn for the beauty of a long summer's day, walking along a dusty country lane surrounded by fields of burnished wheat? How about wide-open pastures ringed with towering pines and leafy oaks? Is your idea of heaven exchanging city for small-town life and sharing a cozy country home with the man you love?

Good, because that's what happened to me, and that's what this book is all about. Although I'd thought about turning in my high heels for a pair of boots often enough, I didn't know how to go about it. I hadn't expected to meet and fall in love with a country man or to have my life turned around—all within a few months' time. I did have a few qualms about exchanging my fast-paced city career for life on a hundred-acre farm, but that was seven years and a lifetime ago. Since then I've learned a lot about country men, country women, and Country Ways.

Are you in a place in your life where you consider having a loving relationship a priority? Do you dream of long walks at sunset with the man you love? Would you consider changing your life to follow such a dream? Then turn the page and get ready to embark on a journey that will lead you to the life you've been dreaming of—get ready for Country Ways.

A Word to the Wary

Before you jump into *Country Ways,* you may be wondering if there really are country men interested in a committed relationship and, if there are, why they aren't already taken. Well, they're here, and they are available. Here are just a few reasons why:

Single country men tend to stay in the country because there's a long tradition of handing down farms and ranches to the men who work the land. Some families have lived on the same ranch for generations and intend to continue into the next. But while single guys are content to stay in the country, single women often leave. If they don't meet a sweetheart growing up (or if they get divorced), they may feel restless. These women gravitate toward cities for what seem like good reasons—more jobs, convenience, entertainment, shopping, and seemingly plenty of places to meet men. But you and I know meeting them isn't enough—you want to meet men who are interested in having a committed relationship or getting married. Although they may be hard to find in the city, believe me, the country offers a *great* selection of these men!

Of course, some of the available men in the country have been married before—divorce does exist even here in the country. But when country men get divorced, they really want to get remarried. They're looking for a helpmate—a woman who's just a little bit country or one who's interested in making Country Ways part of her future. And while country men want to meet the woman of their dreams, they just don't have time to search the city for a woman who *might* consider moving to the country. They'd like to find that special woman within a twenty-mile radius of home, so it makes good sense for you to be right in their backyard if you're interested in the kind of man I'm talking about.

I hope I've changed what may have been an initial hesitation to an attitude of full speed ahead. I want to help you find the *right* man, one who'll be a good husband, partner, and father—a country man!

Section One

Where and How to Find a Country Man

CHAPTER 1

What Are Country Ways?

It's pretty much a given that New Yorkers have a different lifestyle from people in California or Iowa. Some of those differences are obvious, like the landscape, buildings, and whether you take the freeway or subway to work. Other differences, like how people talk and act, may be a little harder to explain, but we know they're there. Taking the analogy a step further, it isn't hard to imagine that the culture of city and country might be quite different, too. When I talk about "Country Ways," I'm referring to the culture and customs of small-town, farm, and ranch life.

There's a warmth and richness to country life that harkens back to a time when people were close, whether neighbors, families, or friends. Country life naturally brings people together, rather than keeping them apart, and I think that's because all of us have at least one thing in common. We were either born to, or have chosen to be, *country.*

Country Ways is a return to the basics—love, courage, and commitment, working hard, loving wisely, and enjoying life to the fullest. Country life is a more authentic, simpler way to live that's measured more by the cycles of nature than the clock, and that means most people are on the same schedule. If you're branding cattle or helping mares foal, your neighbors are probably doing the same. Gardens are sowed in early spring, and the last vegetables are picked in late fall. When you're getting ready to harvest wheat and see storm clouds on the horizon, everyone hustles to help. Neighbors, both far and wide, have a lot in common out in the country, and that brings them together.

Country Ways means knowing we're in this way of life together, that we can count on each other, and that we *want* to. It doesn't matter whether you have enough money to hire extra help or if you *are* the hired help, everybody gets mud on their boots. That connection is the heart of Country Ways. It's the same whether you're just starting out or have the biggest ranch in the county. Being neighborly comes with the territory, and the feeling's as natural as the land we work and the families we cherish.

Country Ways is seeing people for who they are rather than what they wear. In the city I'm often drawn to notice the little things that people do to call attention to themselves, to assert that they're individuals. That sort of thing is alien to country life. My neighbor simply is who he is, and dressing him in a $200 sport coat won't change him a bit—and we both know that. In the country we go for substance over image and realize value isn't always measured by a man's wallet.

Country living creates a partnership between you and your man, both in life and love. You're both responsible for the relationship, the farm, ranch, home-based business, or whatever it is you do. You get equal billing, credit, rewards, *and* hard knocks. Country Ways is being down-to-earth, accountable for your actions, working hard, and loving strong. There isn't much room for "prima donna" types, and princesses need not apply.

Country Ways means letting the little things go and finding ways to work the big things out because you *need* each other. That may sound like a compromise, and it is, because that's what makes a relationship work. You're making an investment in your life, and every minute counts. You can't have it all your own way, but neither can he or anyone else. Instead you find a middle ground and work from there.

I've found that country men will do almost anything for you if they see love reflected in your eyes. In other words, your reaction to his behavior reaffirms those loving feelings. Simple, really. Country men crave your respect and admiration and are willing to do a lot to earn it. They don't want flattery, they want appreciation, a smile, and a thank-you.

In return, your country man will love, cherish, and encourage you in everything you do. He'll cheer accomplishments, forget failures, and kiss your disappointments away. Does that sound like the guy you've been looking for? Are you willing to do what it takes to find *and* keep him? Then you're up to the challenge of Country Ways!

CHAPTER 2

A Tale of Two Women

Now that you've got the general idea, how do you go about getting your little piece of country *and* the guy to go with it? Well, that all depends on whether your dream is to move to the country, to find your true love, or both. Which comes first, the man or the move?

The answers to those questions (and many more) depend on you and what you're *reasonably* comfortable doing. I say *reasonably* because change does create discomfort, and we're talking about making some pretty substantial changes. Change also requires courage. My country man occasionally refers to an old adage that defines courage as "the ability to sustain the tension without resorting to fight or flight." I'd agree, adding that courage means standing your ground when challenged, to find ways around the problems life throws your way, and not giving up or giving in.

Change certainly involves tension, as well as pushing the edges of your personal comfort zone. All these things take courage. A good way to bolster your courage is to gather as much information as you can. The more you know about a given situation, the better able you are to handle yourself. So let's start with something you know—yourself. There are a few basic questions you should ask yourself before really beginning your quest:

Are you ready for a change this big?

Are you willing to devote a few months to finding out?

What, if anything, is holding you back?

What can you do about those obstacles?

If you're hesitant, stop and remind yourself that your goal is to find the man of your dreams. We both know that sitting on the sofa isn't going to take you where you want to go. What you need is a change. You don't have to do it all at once. Take small bites and chew real hard.

Now, let's talk about two different types of women. The first is interested in the kind of man I've described and hasn't found him in the city. She enjoys the country but probably never thought of moving there, let alone living on a ranch or farm. She may not even be particularly fond of animals. And she may have seen country living as a dream outside her reach, a way of life she could never create on her own. This woman may be self-confident and independent, quiet and shy, or anywhere in between. Let's call this woman Anne.

Anne should look for her country man while continuing with her present career and lifestyle. Finding him won't happen overnight (remember—anything worth having is worth waiting for), and she'll have to be patient. Anne should spend two or three months getting to know people in her first "target area" (see chapter 3).

That doesn't mean she'll find a special man in two months, but she'll have met a few eligible men and know whether she wants to spend more time in that community. If not, she should choose another target area and start over. Remember, this process takes time. For Anne, finding her special man is priority number one. Once that happens, everything else will fall into place.

Now let's consider a woman who has a different perspective—we'll call her Susan. Susan has already decided she wants to leave the city and has several very good reasons—lifestyle issues, a desire to raise animals, train horses, write, grow herbs, pursue a career as a naturalist photographer, start a home-based business, or any number of things suited to country life. If she has children, she may want to raise them in a small, close-knit community or even try "home schooling" (an alternative, state-sanctioned program where the parent supervises and teaches within the context of an organized home-schooling group).

Susan may have transferable employment skills, the ability to telecommute to her present job, or other financial resources. She hopes to find a man to share her life, but that's not her first priority. Susan may want to consider moving to the country *before* finding that special man. Her priorities in selecting target areas will likely be different from Anne's and may include business, economic, and other demographic factors.

The process of fitting into the community, along with the advice found in *Country Ways,* will help Susan recognize or create opportunities to meet eligible men. Since finding her love match isn't Susan's top priority, she's also got time on her side. That's a valuable tool she can use to her advantage. It takes time to establish a home or business or settle the kids in new schools, but that doesn't mean Susan should wait until her new life is in order before meeting men or making friends with country women (see chapter 7). You never know which door may lead to heaven!

Although neither of these descriptions may fit you exactly, I think you can see the difference between women like Anne and Susan. Both courses of action I've described have their share of advantages and obstacles, and both can be wildly successful. It's all up to you. Choose the road that suits you best, hop in the driver's seat, and start your engine!

CHAPTER 3

Try a Small Town on for Size

Whether you intend to move as soon as possible or meet the right man and then make your move, your first task is to choose a location to focus on. If you live in a large city, there are probably a dozen nearby communities that would be considered "country." That means outside the commute zone and *beyond* the suburban sprawl that surrounds our cities. Once you've passed suburbia and traveled about another hour, you're most likely in the country. It may take under an hour—you'll know you're there when you see farms, ranches, animals, and wide-open spaces. Your options will include both small villages and larger towns. Some will focus on agriculture or art, while others will have a pretty town square or an impressive courthouse flanked by attractive gardens and a wide expanse of lawn.

The first thing you need to do is decide on a "target area" that includes a town with a population of between two and fifteen thousand.

Look at areas with population centers of between two and ten thousand if you want a close-knit community. If a strong economic base is on your list of essentials, focus on towns with a population between ten and fifteen thousand. Towns are established communities, with social networks that serve the surrounding forty- or fifty-mile area. That's a lot of territory and people to cover, and you should spend a month or two doing just that. Each community will have things you like and other things you don't. You can obtain a variety of information about communities through the local Chamber of Commerce, mayor's office, nearby community college, extension office of the state university, library, bookstores, and individual civic and business leaders. Consider, too, whether the town has a cultural or art agency or is part of the national "Main Street" movement focusing on downtown redevelopment.

When choosing an area, make a "can't do without" list.

Be careful that you don't limit yourself too much, but be realistic: if you can't do without a cultural center or a homeopathic doctor, you'll have to cross certain areas off your list. Keep in mind there *will* be things you'll miss. For me, it was a large, well-stocked bookstore. On the other hand, our library system far exceeded my expectations. I can call up the regional library's card catalog on my computer, browse by subject, author, or title, check out books, and have them shipped to me free of charge.

Your "must have" list may include education, the cost of living, real estate, housing, or the local economy. While it's true you can't build a community on retail, you can build it on tourism, agriculture, and a factory or two. Many small towns are as proud of their industry as they are of their agricultural base or cultural center.

It's a good idea to make sure the area meets your needs *before* you fall in love with a town—or a man. You might also want to make a point of selecting at least two target areas to make the most of your options. Of course, my personal experience is that when you find the right man, everything else (as my country guy promised me) is "just details."

Once you've chosen your first target area, subscribe to the local newspaper. Arrange for a mail subscription and if that's not possible, find out where to obtain the newspaper locally. Small-town newspapers are usually published midweek, so if you can't pick up a copy till the weekend, make arrangements to have one set aside.

This is your best resource for discovering the economic, religious, and political climate of any small town. You can also catch a hint of the *flavor* of the area by reading the "Letters to the Editor," feature articles, and columns written by local people. It's important to read the paper front to back—this is also your weekly road map for finding where the men are! You'll find clues in the weekly calendar of local events and articles about people and upcoming events.

Check out the "Public Notices" section of the classifieds for notices of public hearings and government auctions—both excellent places to meet people.

There's sure to be something going on in and around town on the weekends, so make plans to get to town early Saturday morning. I also suggest you go alone, if not your first trip, then as soon as you're comfortable. Girlfriends are fun, but men will find you much more approachable if you're by yourself. You might want to consider spending the night in a bed-and-breakfast or a motel. Although both will probably be locally owned, you'll have a more personal visit at the B&B, which can be an excellent source of information and personal contacts.

Once you've chosen a target area (or two), you're ready to start arranging your schedule to spend time in the country. I suggest you take the time to discover the differences *and* the people in each target area you choose. Since country people are naturally cool to strangers and flatlanders (that's you!), they may need to see you around a time or two before warming up.

When I first moved to the country, I made a point of saying hello to everyone I came into contact with, whether on the street, in a store, or at a community function. Whenever I got the chance, I shook hands and introduced myself. Making the first move goes a long way toward bridging the gap between longtime residents and newcomer.

Another hint: Don't volunteer that you're city bred.

Some parts of the country have a "them and us" attitude about city people moving in and "taking over." Whether that's founded on real or imagined problems is another issue. The point is, if you're real friendly and down-to-earth, they may not notice just how city you are! Whether it's a rainy spring, long, sun-drenched summer, lingering autumn, or snowy winter, any time will do to make a start. Every season has both challenges and rewards. Get to know your part of the country through them all!

CHAPTER 4

Where the Men Are

Although it is possible to meet men just about anywhere, the country affords some unique opportunities. None of them are anywhere near a "singles scene," and that's the point. You're looking for places to talk to men about everyday things, not to get a date for next week. That will come later. But in order to take advantage of the meeting places the country has to offer, familiarize yourself with the following top choices for meeting men.

1. *Estate auctions.* There's usually one or two to choose from every weekend, spring through late summer, all within an hour's drive of the small town of your choice. Estate auctions are for men as shopping malls are for women. They go whether they're buying or just browsing. Estate auctions advertise in the local newspaper and list major items to be sold.

- Head for auctions listing heavy equipment and machinery, tools, farm and ranching gear, and saddles and tack.

- Dress casually. You'll be tramping around in dirt and grass, but you'll also want to blend in and look pretty.

Wear a simple summer dress, jeans, or shorts and a cute T-shirt. And be sure and wear comfortable walking shoes—the auctioneer and the bidders go where the tools, equipment, and tack are, and you don't want to be left behind. Serious bidders arrive at least an hour before the scheduled auction to check things out, so be sure to arrive early.

- This pre-auction time is a perfect opportunity to strike up a conversation with a man.

One easy way to do this is to ask a question or two about things that are going on the auction block. Remember, he should *correctly* assume you're there to bid on goods, so stick to those topics.

Country estate auctions run two ways, depending on how much they have to auction off: one auctioneer "calls" everything, usually starting outdoors and leaving the household goods and furniture till last, or two auctioneers "call," one outside, the other inside. If two auctions are going on simultaneously, you may be inclined to go inside for the household goods auction. Don't do that, because any man you meet may very well be married! Trust me—the eligible men will be outside.

Don't make the mistake of bidding on farm tools so you can turn them into planters or ornaments.

I promise there's a farmer or rancher in the crowd who will lose his chance to buy something he would use, and he'll lose that chance because you'll outbid him every time. (And for good reason—antiques bought at auction prices are a good buy.) Just think how you'd feel if you outbid a farmer for a cream separator (which he needed), and he came to your house a few months later and saw it transformed into a pleasingly arranged planter.

Remember, you're there to make a good impression and to introduce yourself to the community. Country folk respect the past as well as the future, and you don't want to label yourself one of those city women who throw their money away (or who turn perfectly good farm equipment into planters). That won't get you the kind of attention you want. Bidding once or twice and then bowing out gracefully *will.*

Here's another tip to help you fit in. Auctioneers will occasionally ask bidders to start the action at $5 (or $10 or $50). Never fall for that trick!

Patience is important at an auction. Those in the know, wait. Those who don't, jump in with a bid. The auctioneer will come down on that number until someone finally jumps in. Don't be the first bidder, or if the auctioneer is down to $5, put up three fingers, not five. This means you're bidding $3, not the $5 the auctioneer is asking, and shows you know what you're doing.

2. *Livestock auctions.* Check the ads for auctions where livestock are bought and sold. You may think that seems odd, but you can tell a lot about a man by the way he acts around animals. When I first visited my country man's farm, I saw a goat with only three legs and asked what had happened. He told me he'd seen the goat at the auction, and just when he was thinking she was headed for a sad demise, the goat turned and gave him what he called a "sad, wistful gaze." He said he knew it was silly, but he brought her home and named her Peg-of-My-Heart. So if you happen to go to a livestock auction and see a man buying a sad-looking animal, you might ask him why. I wonder where I'd be now if some smart, single woman had done that when my guy made the only bid for Peg.

3. *State university extension conferences and workshops.* Most small towns have a "county extension agent." The agent works with the state university system to organize and hold all sorts of educational activities—anything from a ten-week course on timber management to a Saturday art fair.

Pick up a copy of the extension office's monthly newsletter and choose from dozens of possibilities.

Take special note of classes that run four to six weeks. That gives you an even better opportunity to get to know that special guy! Gwen, the receptionist at my doctor's office, met her husband when she took a six-week master gardener course in a town thirty miles away. The course is offered twice a year in different locations, and she couldn't attend when it was offered in her town. That stroke of "bad luck" turned into the best thing that ever happened to her! She and her honey set up housekeeping a year later and recently tied the knot.

Here's a sampling of our regional offerings for March: Master Gardener Series Orientation, Wool Growers Association Lambing School, Small Farm Conference, Cheese-Making Workshop, Livestock Growers' Meeting, Dairy Farm Management Workshop, Naturalist Writers' Workshop, Fiber Fair, Beef Producers' Conference, Small Woodlands Marketing Workshop, Organic Fruit Workshop, Edible Landscape Seminar, Leadership Series (for people involved in community groups or serving on local boards), Master Food Preserver Series, and Tree Pruning Techniques. Need I say more?

4. *Downtown cafés:* Every small town has at least one, some two or three. Don't bother with restaurants located on the outskirts of town or along the highway. Those are for tourists. You want to dine with the locals!

- Have breakfast at the local café every time you come to town, and do sit at the counter—that's where the single men are.

- Get to know the waitress.

Be sure to tell her how much you like the area and that you're thinking of relocating. She'll know everybody and everything that's going on in town—an invaluable source of information. She may also have a single brother, uncle, or son!

5. *Public hearings on land use issues.* This is a subject of

high interest to landowners. Public hearings are listed in the front of the classified section of the local newspaper. They're always well attended. Real estate developers, large landowners, and people in the market for small parcels will all be there. Public hearings are where local issues take center stage.

- Show up early and introduce yourself to a few people.

- The easiest icebreaker is to talk about the subject of the hearings.

People will be adamantly for or against, so ask all the questions you want, but don't take sides. This is also a good opportunity to learn about local politics. The debate will be heated (land use issues always are), and you're sure to find people eager to discuss their point of view. Don't be surprised if someone asks why you're attending the hearing. People in small towns frequently ask newcomers questions you'd feel uncomfortable asking them. It's not that they're nosy, but if you're interested in their town, they're going to be interested in you. You can easily address the curiosity factor by saying you're looking at a nearby piece of property or you want to know how the county feels about growth.

6. *The library.* Our library maintains a calendar of events with something going on several nights a week. There are local speakers, presentations on history and culture, art shows, slide presentations, and discussion and writers' groups. Most evening events are preceded

by a social hour, so you'll have plenty of time to meet people.

Community events are a very good opportunity for single people to find each other. Two more places I'd recommend are high school sports (especially if you have children) and church. Be sure to check the banks and post office for notices about community dinners and fraternal lodge open-house nights. If the event is advertised, you're invited, along with everybody else in town. Country folk are naturally friendly, and you should be, too.

Chapter 5

Saturday Night Special

It's Saturday night, you're in the small town of your choice, and you've discovered a gold mine—a place with both music and men. (I'll talk later about how to do this, but first I wanted to get your attention!) How do you take the next step and meet that handsome, hardworking, small-town guy standing on the other side of the room? Is it better to walk up and say hello or wait for him to take the first step? Do you act aggressive or shy, friendly or reserved, be yourself or impress him with a city girl's version of country?

He already knows you're new in town (otherwise he'd know you), which gives you both a reason to introduce yourself and something to talk about. This is a good chance to ask questions, while giving him the opportunity to offer to be your personal tour guide!

Men like to feel needed. They want to be your knight in shining armor. By all means, let him rescue you—even if it's only from your single status.

By making this first and *apparently* casual first move, you've also accomplished something else. Country men are generally shy, and in one fell swoop you've given him an opportunity to spend time with you without making it a "date." Who knows, after a few hours you may decide he'd make a better friend than love interest. Remember, though, he will always live here. You will see him again. Don't alienate anybody.

It's quite acceptable to talk to him first, but go slow and take it easy.

If you're too aggressive, you'll either scare him off or give him the wrong impression—that you find it easy to approach men and do it all the time. You want him to think he's special. And who knows, he may be. You just want a chance to find that out. It's perfectly acceptable to wander up and say hello.

Better yet, have a few questions ready so you'll have something interesting to talk about.

Start with something easy—what you already have in common. Choose from among the following: the town, specifics about the area such as the mountains, a scenic river, animals, wildlife, or agriculture. Ask questions about annual events like the county fair, rodeo, community days, or the spring art festival (since you've done your homework, you should already know a little about these things). Talk about the local economy, jobs, tourism—it's even okay to talk about the weather. In fact, country folk talk about the weather a lot.

Country life revolves around the seasons and the natural ebb and flow of nature. It's quite reasonable to talk about something that has such an impact over your life. Talking about the weather is an ingrained country habit, so don't think a man is boring if he talks about last year's rainfall or snow levels. Besides, this is your information-gathering phase, and you might get some good tips. Gardeners are as interested in rainfall and soil conditions as cooks are in vegetable gardens—and the weather affects both. The cycles of nature are all played out in the country, and you want to be part of it all.

It's not a good idea to ask him to dance, not even after you've been introduced.

It's not a given that he can dance, and he might be embarrassed to admit he can't. Tapping your toe to the music and smiling is enough of an invitation. If he doesn't get the hint, take a wait-and-see attitude. Don't assume he isn't interested. I know you've got an agenda, but he's got time on his hands. Remember, country folk are traditional. If you interpret that as being *slow,* try to leave your impatience in the city and readjust your clock to country. That may seem simple, but it's harder than it sounds. You may be dying to meet a country guy, but he probably won't "chat you up" or ask you to dance until he's seen you around a time or two.

Now, how to find that Saturday night special place!

Check the local newspaper and stores for flyers advertising your choices for night life.

This brings up the issue of bars and taverns, so let's tackle that first. I don't recommend them as a place to meet men, but that's only partially an issue of alcohol. My country man and I enjoy an occasional beer in town, but we go together. I wouldn't go alone. You don't want to be categorized as a "loose woman" (see chapter 13), and like it or not, frequenting bars *may* give you that reputation. Initial impressions are important. Keep in mind that small-town folks *do* gossip, and that can be both good and bad. Avoid any possible strikes against your city woman image, while encouraging points in favor of Country Ways.

A man who enjoys an occasional beer and game of pool is okay, whether he's city or country. I do have some doubts about a man who considers a bar his second home. You want a hardworking man with ambition, not a man who spends his evenings talking to the town cronies.

There *are* exceptions to the "no bar" rule. Any enterprising proprietor wants local business, and taverns are no different. They'll often have an inexpensive (and early) all-you-can-eat spaghetti or barbecue on weekends and line-dance lessons or a local band to liven up a Saturday night. By all means, go!

Other places for evening socializing are fraternal

organizations (the Grange, Masons, Eagles, Odd Fellows, and the like) and the VFW (Veterans of Foreign Wars). They frequently hold fund-raising or celebration dinners as well as special events. You'll see flyers posted around town a few weeks in advance so you'll have plenty of time to plan your weekends.

If you can't spend the weekend away from home, all is not lost. Remember, country evenings end pretty early. You should have time for some Saturday night fun and stay awake long enough for a safe drive home.

Try to go alone on most of your country excursions.

Men generally find it easier to approach women who are alone rather than trying to choose one from among a cluster. Women seem to find it difficult to be on their own, but I suggest you take a hard look at your goals and your game plan. Take a deep breath and take the plunge. It's not nearly as difficult as you might think.

Country folk are hospitable and go out of their way to make newcomers feel comfortable. If you're alone, it won't be for long, because someone's sure to strike up a conversation. Be friendly and talk to as many people as you can. Country men have families, and they probably live nearby. What better way to meet a man than through his grandmother, uncle, or child? Yes, *child.* Don't be surprised to see children at almost any country social event, and that child just may have a single dad. Remember, you never know whom your country contacts may turn up.

Some social events will take place in a large room or hall, with long tables set up and five or six chairs on each side. This is considered "open seating."

Wander around for a while before deciding where to sit. Don't choose an empty table. Find one with a few empty seats and "hover" nearby for a moment.

In the flash of an eye, you'll probably be invited to join the table. If the people already seated are in the midst of a conversation, it's quite all right to interrupt with a smile and ask, "Is this seat taken?" Of course, it won't be, so sit right down and introduce yourself!

By the end of the evening you'll have met some interesting people and know more about what's going on nearby. Make sure to tell everyone how much you like the town, the open spaces, river, mountains, Main Street, or whatever you think is special. Remember, relationships are your key to success in the country. Every person you meet is an opportunity to find that special man; everything you learn about the town, and everyone in it, will go a long way toward making a smooth transition from city to country life.

CHAPTER 6

Main Street, the Heart of Every Small Town

I've always loved the glass snow scenes in the stores at Christmas time—the ones filled with tiny miniatures. Turn the glass upside-down and watch tiny snowflakes fall on quaint English towns, Santa's workshop, or a sleigh and eight tiny reindeer. For one brief moment it's as if you're catching a glimpse into another world. A small country town reminds me of those miniatures.

If you walk down Main Street at suppertime, you can catch a glimpse inside the lives of country folk. It's that magical time between dusk and nightfall, when the family's all together, that you see how people really live. Is she fixing dinner while he reads the paper? Is she reading to the kids while *he* cooks? Are they watching television, playing Monopoly or The Farming Game? (This blatant plug is for the neighbor who invented and markets The Farming Game and is another example of Country Ways. We help each other out whenever we can.)

Country folk also enjoy spending time outdoors, whether it's backyard wedding receptions, barbecues, tossing a Frisbee, playing a game of horseshoes, or watching the kids play in a plastic wading pool.

Walking along the streets of our town is a good way to meet people and should definitely be part of your game plan.

A friendly hello and a question or two about a front-yard garden or garage sale could well turn into an invitation to enjoy a glass of iced tea and conversation on the porch.

There's a lot going on in the country during the "growing season" (spring through fall). Saturday markets are usually held downtown or in one of the church parking lots. They start early in the morning and run until early afternoon.

Wear comfortable, casual clothes and bring a large net or canvas bag to store your purchases of organic and farm produce, fresh flowers, handmade soap, jams and jellies, honey, flavored mustards and vinegars, and one-of-a-kind crafts.

Depending on the size of the market, you can easily spend several hours shopping, meeting, and talking to farmers, craftsmen, artisans, and townsfolk. This is a great way to get a "feel" for a town and the people who live there. Since there'll be both city and country people at the market, pay attention to their clothing to know who's local and who's not. Country folk will have spent the early hours getting ready for the market, and their clothes will reflect that hard work. In any case, the people *selling* will be country, the buyers some of each.

Communities hold weekend fairs to celebrate regional specialties and interests, whether it's huckleberries, wine and art, or blue grass, jazz, or country music. If you've been reading the local newspaper, you probably saw an article asking for volunteers for everything from setup and cleanup operations, to taking tickets, to manning local booths. This is an ideal way to meet people.

Call the contact person listed in the newspaper and volunteer.

Local folks will see you as a person who's interested in helping the community and someone with a "can do" attitude. What a great way to introduce yourself!

I've known Laura for a couple of years. She met her man when she volunteered to set out signs directing cars into a parking lot at a small harvest festival. Mrs. Holcomb, an elderly nearsighted woman, nearly ran her over, then felt so bad she insisted on taking Laura to the local high school booth for a glass of iced tea. Dean, a handsome single dad, was manning the booth. He managed to keep her with him for over an hour, then escorted her to the harvest festival dinner.

Within a few months, they were *keeping company* (see chapter 15).

Country men are particularly interested in events celebrating history, like Civil War reenactments, gatherings for enthusiasts of trains, steam engines, or paddle wheelers, or demonstrations of old skills, like blacksmithing, metal-, or woodworking. Be sure to take advantage of these opportunities. Go, whether you're interested in blacksmithing or not. If you are, so much the better, but you *are* interested in meeting people!

One nearby town holds an annual threshing bee, an old-time celebration of the wheat harvest. It's no coincidence that over half the attendees are men. There are steam-powered threshing machines, living history exhibits, blacksmithing and knife-making demonstrations, arts and crafts booths, and a Saturday night barbecue. A walk down Main Street during that weekend will find locals as well as people from neighboring communities talking over a beer or ice cream soda.

It won't be as difficult as you think to join a conversation. Try something like "I'm new in town. Could you tell me where I might find a telephone [or water fountain, drugstore, town hall, or grocery store]?" While in the city you might get rude stares, in the country, folk will always respond. The conversation may be short, but you never know where it may lead.

Every small community has a Fourth of July bang-up parade and celebration lasting long into the night. Some towns go all out with a steak feed, country western bands, street dancing, and fireworks just after dusk. Main Street is *the* place to be on Independence

Day. Country folk are proud of their celebrations and welcome visitors to join in the fun!

The county fair and rodeo may be held at the fairgrounds but Main Street merchants get in the act, too. There are sidewalk sales, lemonade and ice cream stands, music on the lawn of the courthouse, and streets blocked off for a small carnival for the kids. You'll find cowboys galore at the rodeo, as well as events like barrel racing, calf roping, team penning, and branding. There's livestock showmanship, trials, and auctions where you'll meet people interested in animals. You could also check out exhibits that exemplify country life—crops, horticulture, food preservation, crafts and hobbies, gardening, and, of course, livestock. You may meet people from nearby towns and discover another "target area" to explore!

Fairs and rodeos are family activities and, if you have kids, may be a good opportunity to expose them to Country Ways. There are so many things to do and see, so many people to meet—children won't stand in the way of your talking with a country guy. If he happens to have *his* kids around, so much the better! More than one couple have met while waiting in line for pony rides or separating their precious little tomboys from a swing set dispute.

Country folk celebrate the lingering days of autumn by decorating with nature's bounty. A trip to the garden might turn up colorful gourds, Indian corn, or bright sunflowers a foot or more in diameter! Front porches are transformed into country scenes, complete with bales of hay and bushel baskets piled high with leaves turned shades of red and gold. You may even see a scarecrow dressed in Grandpa's bib overalls, a wide-brimmed straw hat, and a red bandanna.

With Halloween approaching, there's usually friendly rivalry between neighbors vying for the title of "Scariest Haunted House." You're likely to find school carnivals, where you can bob for apples, throw darts at balloons, and win a stuffed teddy bear. There's even the possibility of ending the evening with a moonlight hayride!

The holidays are a time for gift giving, and that means shopping. Church and community bazaars will offer handcrafted items for young and old, holiday decorations, wooden toys, jams, jellies, hand-knit socks, quilts, and a whole lot more. Craftsmen will be there, as well as organizers and local folk looking to buy gifts for their families.

- Introduce yourself, be friendly, and compliment the craftsmen. They probably live right in town.

- A conversational tip: It's especially easy to strike up a conversation with an interesting man during the holidays. Just ask him if he still believes in Santa Claus!

Our town holds a Christmas competition for the best decorated house and yard. Thousands of strands of colored bulbs outline rafters, windows, and doors, and tiny lights shine from bushes and tall oak trees along every street in town. You can find those contests in the city, too. But in the country it's the neighbors who do the choosing, not a group of socialites or elected officials. Spirits are high as neighbors bundle up to go outside and join the fun. If you're just visiting, the holiday festivities give you a perfect opportunity to talk to people!

Why not come to town and join in? The night air is crisp and clear, the moon a buttery yellow. Snow is piled high on the sides of every street, and the school's baseball diamond is carpeted in white. Carolers sing "Jingle Bells" and "Silent Night." Neighbors hand out cookies and mugs of hot apple cider, hoping to tempt you to vote their house the "Best Decorated." Help celebrate when the winner is announced!

Does that seem like something out of a fairy tale? Can you imagine yourself walking down the street, checking out the houses decked in holiday finery and trimmed with lights? Can you see yourself chatting with people, enjoying the camaraderie and cheer of the season? If you listen closely, you'll hear laughter and the singing of carolers. You may even notice the scent of cinnamon in the apple cider. I don't know about you, but I wish we could both be there right now!

You might think outsiders wouldn't be welcome, but you'd be wrong. Country people are proud of their towns, their kids, and their communities. If you're sincere about wanting to join them, they'll be pleased to have you. You're sure to meet people when you take in the lighting displays, go to craft bazaars, or attend the school holiday pageant. All you have to do is join in the fun!

A sense of community may be hard to find in the city, but it's easy in the country. Just look around you. Visit the local craft shop to take lessons from country artists, or browse the aisles for locally made, one-of-a-kind gifts. Walk into the harness shop, where the air is cool and heavy with the rich smell of leather and sawdust. Listen to wranglers shooting the breeze while picking up fifty-pound sacks of grain at the feed store. You may find what you're looking for at the five-and-dime, the secondhand store, the barber or beauty shop. Community can be found most anyplace, but the *heart* of any town can be found on Main Street.

One final note: The shops on Main Street are likely to be closed on Sundays and after six in the evenings. Shopkeepers want to be with their families, too. Once you get used to the change, you won't mind a bit. While you may think nonstop shopping is a convenience you don't want to give up, consider whether it's time well spent. Organizing your shopping into one or two segments each week gives you something invaluable in return: the precious commodity of time. Time to spend however you choose—with your beau, family, friends, or simply at home. Whether it's relaxing or working at whatever suits your fancy, you've managed to add a few hours to your week *and* your country life!

CHAPTER 7

Country Women as Allies

There's more than just small-town living waiting for you in the country. There's time to redefine relationships, including those with women who will become your friends and staunchest supporters. Don't discount country women because you think they're different. You have a lot to learn from these women, and you have a part to play in sharing your own skills and talents, too.

Country women are important to your acceptance by the community, your happiness, and your success. Don't forget, these women have brothers, uncles, and nephews. Country women know everything about everybody and are one of your best sources on which country men you want to meet. They can steer you in the right direction and introduce you to the right people, or they can make your transition from city to country difficult, if not downright impossible. It's all up to you.

First, there are a few "threshold tests" you should address from your very first day scouting your "target area." The most important involves respect. City dwellers have a tendency to lump people into categories, and country seems to get lumped in with "quaint, simple, and unsophisticated." Yet in reality country women are none of those things. They are smart, courageous, understanding, patient, and persistent. They are jack-of-all-trades and masters of others. When the electricity goes out with a winter storm, they're adept at both entertaining children and fixing a meal over a wood fire—in the fireplace, if necessary.

Do not assume country women are unsophisticated, and do not judge them by their clothes.

Don't make the mistake of thinking (and saying) that what this quaint little town needs is a nice dress shop—a serious and frequently made misstep. Not only will you alienate women by suggesting they don't know how to dress, but the women I know would never buy their going-out attire in town anyway. They much prefer an excuse to drive to the city, go out for lunch, and shop the afternoon away once in a while! Country life may be idyllic, but city getaways are fun, too. Don't forfeit your chance for close friendships with country women by giving them the impression you think city chic is better than country—that could be a *fatal* mistake.

Meeting country women is the easy part, so that's where we'll begin.

Start by attending classes and activities with a decidedly "female" appeal.

Things like fiber arts (the art of using fiber in creative ways, like hand spinning, weaving, felting, quilting, fabric manipulation and embellishment, tapestries, and so forth), craftwork, gardening, and cooking. But don't stop there. You'll find women at seminars on everything from woodland management and sheep and cattle ranching to timber frame and hay bale construction. You'll find them at church, the library, senior center, Chamber of Commerce, community action groups, fraternal organizations, and schools. If you enjoy the outdoors, look for groups focused on things like archery, canoeing, birdwatching, hiking, and wilderness survival. Even better, join the local Search & Rescue, which is usually sponsored by the sheriff's office. Although the majority of members will be men, you'll find women there, too.

Here's another tip: Make an appointment to see a country dentist or doctor for some minor problem or checkup.

This will give you a chance to meet the women in the front office, the bookkeeper, nurses, and dental technicians. When I told my dental hygienist I was writing *Country Ways,* she mentioned her brother's plight—he's a thirty-eight-year-old farmer and a widowed single dad who'd love to meet a woman interested in country living. He wouldn't mind an extra kid or two, either. Some women might think that sounds like a lot to take on, but it might be the answer to your dreams. It's important to get acquainted with any-and-everybody. You never know who's going to be an important link in your chain of contacts.

If you have children, introduce them to 4-H, a great club for children ages six to nineteen that focuses on rural activities.

The 4-H stands for "Head (clear thinking), Hands (service), Heart (loyalty), and Health (better living)." Activities within 4-H include a tremendous variety of learning opportunities on everything from raising and showing animals, to cooking and computer basics, to woodworking and public speaking. If you don't have kids, go to the meetings anyway. Just tell the instructors you need *really* basic instruction. The teachers may or may not be women, but it's a great opportunity to meet moms dropping their kids off or waiting to pick them up.

You'll also meet women with an interest in live theater and the arts as well as gardening and cooking. My local fiber arts group made a day of driving eighty miles to attend a book signing by the author of one of our favorite knitting books. Another group spent the day in a nearby city attending an exhibit on Chinese art. Many country women are well educated and well read. Some operate home-based businesses or call the shots on ranch management. Others are happy to stay home and care for their men, home, and families. It takes all kinds, whether in the city or the country, and there's plenty of room for you!

Make friends with women of all ages.

Country folk embrace and nurture the link between generations, both to teach the young and to seek out the wisdom of the elder. Building a web of interconnected relationships with country women will provide you with companionship, advice, help, and encouragement. Of course, you'll also *give* all those things in return. Although there are differences in the cultures of city and country, women can connect on many different levels. Whether it's family, home, relationships, hobbies, job, or career, explore possible friendships with every woman you meet. That's how to start building that web of relationships that is the hallmark of country life.

Country Ways means sticking together instead of competing, and that applies to women as much as men. That's very different from city attitudes, where competition for jobs, as well as men, is a given. There's a sense of community, a definite "we're in this together" attitude among country women that's difficult to find in the city. It comes from sharing the same struggles and problems, joys and heartaches. You may have that with a few of your friends now, but imagine being part of such a circle with dozens of women. Talk about empowerment! You will want to be part of this circle, but admittance is *not* a given.

Country women may hold you at arm's length for a while. They've met quite a few city gals who've looked down their noses at country. It will be up to you to convince them you're eager to join their ranks. Once they've seen you around a while, and you've helped out at a community event or two, they'll come around.

Getting to know country women is an important step in reaching your goals, so be sure to make it part of your game plan.

It isn't unusual for a club or group to include a "pot luck" meal with their meetings. Some groups, like Master Gardeners, even make pot luck meetings a "show and tell," including sharing recipes and tips for using the bounty from their gardens. Everyone brings a dish to share and their own eating utensils (napkins and paper plates are usually provided). Bring a main dish, salad, or dessert. A good rule of thumb is to bring enough to feed ten people.

These are perfect opportunities to exhibit gourmet cooking skills or to use a simple recipe if that's more your style. Remember, these women have single, eligible friends. They'll want to introduce you around once they know you value their menfolk. To a lot of country women, that means cooking. Quite literally, the proof is in the pudding—and if you make a good one, you'll find bachelors' doors flying open! In no time at all you'll have an invitation to visit that new female friend or her bachelor cousin.

When you do visit, ask for the grand tour—not just the house, but the garden and the animals.

I love an excuse to show off Emma Rose, our prettiest and smartest Saanen goat. She's learned how to open the gate with her mouth, and when the other goats want the afternoon off, they traipse off to find Emma Rose and have her open the gate for them. We've wondered why the other goats don't learn from watching Emma Rose, but maybe they think it's easier just to go and get her. After all, she *is* the herd queen! It's stories like these that country folk love to share; hearing (and enjoying) them goes a long way toward making you part of the community.

Remember, all this legwork is preparing you for the time you'll meet a country man who interests you. If you're doing your homework, you'll know enough about ranching, farming, or the town to sound and feel as though you belong. This is a giant first step. If you happen to meet that guy right off, don't worry—ask him to steer you in the right direction. If he's the right man, he'll be more than happy to oblige!

Whether you're a feminist or a time-honored traditionalist, there is a sense of oneness between country women that transcends economic and social factors. It has to do with a return to basics, being attuned to nature and the cycle of life that is legitimate in the country and increasingly sought after in the city. As I've mentioned earlier, country life has a rhythm very different from that in the city. It's slower and more *connected.* You need to acknowledge that rhythm and really see the differences between the two cultures. Some differences are drastic, some so subliminal that newcomers don't catch on for a while. Give yourself time to figure it all out.

So take a few classes, attend a talk or two, give people a chance to get to know you.

One word of caution: Wait a while before offering information about your successes.

Not only do you *not* want to sound like you're bragging, you may get asked to teach a class on your area of expertise. And just because you may not have formal training, don't expect to get off the hook. Country folk recognize skills and talent learned the old-fashioned way—by the seat of your pants. Teaching *may* be a good idea, but offering too much information about yourself can backfire.

When I told people I was a published author, I quickly realized how many people in the country want to be writers. When I was asked to judge a local writing contest, I was flattered. After all, volunteering is a good thing. Right? In this case, it wasn't. Criticism is tough to give and even tougher to accept, especially from a newcomer. I made the mistake of stepping on a few toes, and it took me a while to get back on track. When you're new in town, withholding criticism, even when it's asked for, is the better answer.

Volunteer wherever you have skills, talent, or time.

There will be lots of opportunities on the weekends. Try the library, county extension office, churches, museums, petting zoo, community programs, hospital, the senior center—they all operate with a minimum of volunteers. Women make up the core of volunteer operations in the country, and you'll be seen correctly as someone who wants to make a difference in your community, someone who works hard and has a caring nature.

Volunteering is one way to earn that well-deserved

respect and admittance to the community of women. You'll be on the *team.* You'll be the kind of woman a country woman will want to get to know, someone she'll want to be friends with and introduce to that single brother, uncle, or nephew. You've taken an important step along your journey to finding your niche in the country *and* your country man!

CHAPTER 8

Country Make-Over (How to Blend In)

Have you ever been to a cocktail party, dressed to the nines, and noticed a woman wearing ripped jeans and a T-shirt? Your impression of this woman was probably either 1) "Poor thing, no wonder she's alone," 2) "She must have wandered into the wrong party," or 3) neither, because you didn't bother to give her a second thought. We all know first impressions are very important.

When a city woman comes to the country in high heels and slinky satin, she's making a statement. Here's what a country man is liable to think: 1) "There's a woman looking for some *action,*" 2) "Pretty, but way out of my league," or 3) neither, because he won't bother giving her a second thought.

Dressing to impress *will* get you attention, but not

the kind you want. You'll alienate the country women and you won't get a country man for the long term. You may have a few laughs and a good time, but that's not what we're talking about. We're talking about finding love in all the *right* places. We're talking Country Ways.

A country man isn't looking for a fashion model. He's looking for the girl next door. Put your short skirts and expensive angora sweaters in the closet and leave the white high-tops at home. Hundred-dollar designer sneakers don't belong in the country.

Wear comfortable jeans or a soft corduroy skirt, and choose a pretty blouse that brings out the color of your eyes. Flats, walking shoes, or hiking boots are your best bet to fit right in.

Looking the part is important because you'll be *approachable.* He'll feel *comfortable* talking to you, getting to know you, and introducing you to his friends and family. If you look out of place, he may feel you truly are. Country folk tend to get an "attitude" toward flatlanders who both want to fit in *and* cling to their city ways. Well, you can't have it both ways. You've got to choose. We figure the least you can do is dress the part. Otherwise it looks as if you're trying to make some *point,* and that point seems to be that you're better than we are.

We all know it's what's on the inside that really matters, but as I said earlier, impressions are important—especially first ones. If you present a glamorous outside, country folk may never discover your wonderful inside. Dressing as though you already belong tells country people that you have values and expectations similar to their own. That's the first step toward acceptance.

Country folk are down-to-earth, "say what you mean and mean what you say" kinds of people. Besides, if you live in the country, your clothes get dirty! Why ruin a perfectly good pair of high-heeled boots tramping around the countryside? Save them for trips to the city. Country Ways means understanding expensive wrapping paper isn't as important as what's tucked inside the package.

That applies to cosmetics, too. I'm all for making the most of your looks, but remember that *less* is better than more. Let your natural beauty shine through. Makeup can't hold a candle to a healthy glowing complexion, clean shiny hair, and a pretty smile. Again, you want to look as though you belong.

The country look isn't about glamour—no glossy black mascara and ruby red lipstick needed. Instead go for subtle, understated, and approachable. Don't get me wrong—I don't mean dowdy. Just remember that sexy is like beauty in the eye of the beholder, and a country beholder values wholesome over trashy, hands down. But we can't stop here. Country makeovers require altering more than just your appearance. City make-overs are about pushing back the clock—reversing the aging process on your face and body through makeup, facials, body wraps, and even surgery. A country make-over means learning to keep time on your side by changing pace.

For maximum effects, you must slow down and take it easy, both in how you talk and act.

In the city, you're pressed for time and anxious to get on with things, whether it's ordering dinner or asking questions. Country folk generally think city people are brusque, aggressive, and sometimes downright rude. I'm not saying they are, but that is how they're perceived. I think the problem stems from a time warp between city and country. City life is hurried and harried. Country life is slow and smooth.

Before you get your dander up, remember that "hurried and harried" may not be what the doctor ordered and often leads to stress. The best remedy for what ails you may be that "slow and smooth" lifestyle we're talking about. Believe me, I know. When I was leading my fast-paced city life, I had a number of physical ailments that I'd come to accept as "normal." All were related to stress. Within six months of moving to the country, all had disappeared from my life, along with the half dozen bottles of pills I'd kept on my bedside table for years.

You may not have these kinds of problems, but I think you'll be surprised by how much better you'll feel when you slow your pace a bit. Replacing anxiety with calm, deadlines for quality time, and a commute for a long walk at sunset are all by-products of country living. Once you start to recognize this difference in rhythm between city and country, you'll have started the process of adjusting to life in the "past" lane.

Don't criticize how long it takes to get things done or try to hurry everybody up.

Remember, you're in the country, and there's no clock to beat. Work on slowing your pace, your manner of speech, and your expectations.

Remember, also being on a fast track is not necessarily good for you! Immerse yourself in this way of life and try it on for size. That's the only way to decide whether it fits right or whether you need to make a few adjustments. Don't expect to get used to Country Ways in a week or two. Setting your clock to country time takes a while.

CHAPTER 9

The Two-and-Twenty Rule

Bev moved to town a few years ago and had several beaus courting her within a few months. She took her time deciding but finally settled on Mike, a local land developer. Their wedding was held in a small, historic chapel, with the outdoor reception a step away and catered by one of our local restaurants. Bev is a perfect example of the two-and-twenty rule. She's pleasant looking, with shoulder-length hair and big brown eyes. She's also a size twelve or fourteen. Surprised? Don't be.

Generally speaking, country women are more pleasing than perfect, and that brings us to the two-and-twenty rule. Simply put, that means when a woman moves to the country, she gains two points in looks and loses twenty pounds relative to those around her. Now, who can argue with that?

One of the major differences between city and country is the competition. It seems to rear its ugly head just about everywhere, including a woman's chances for meeting eligible men. In the city, competition is tough. In the country, your odds are better. First of all, there aren't as many single women. Second, women so beautiful they could win beauty pageants seem drawn to city lights instead of country nights.

Country men appreciate strong women. Remember, they're looking for someone to help them run the ranch, and that means having both emotional and physical strength. If that's not where your talents or interests lie, that's okay. You don't have to be tough as nails to live in the country. You can be soft as corn silk. Either way, your new life will give you an opportunity to grow, in both body *and* spirit.

Most country men want a woman who's happy. There's nothing more beautiful than a woman with a sunny disposition, one who's content with her life. Physical appearance isn't as important in the country as it is in the city, because window dressing just doesn't mean very much. We're more interested in who you are and what you stand for. It's what's *inside* that really counts. You may not have had the time, or the opportunity, to discover the *real* you. You may have been so busy rushing about that the real you is lost somewhere inside, trying desperately to get out. Now's the time, and the country is the place. With that special man by your side, cheering you on, discovery can be an awesome thing!

You don't have to be a "farm girl," but you should want to be a *country woman.* If you're not working alongside your man, put on a fresh pot of coffee to welcome him home. That's the kind of thing to turn a country man's head. They appreciate the little touches only a woman can bring to their lives. It doesn't matter if you're more rounded than svelte. Being pretty on the inside counts more than pinup girl looks.

Ranching and farming is real—sometimes tough and other times tender. Spending an afternoon in your vegetable garden may leave you sore and aching, while an early morning turn at bottle-feeding orphaned lambs may fill you with peace. Being close to nature will give you opportunities to learn and grow in the space of your own backyard, whether it's a few acres or a thousand. Whether tilling the soil or gazing at a star-filled sky, tending animals or watching eagles soar, there's something new and exciting every day. If the beauty of these new discoveries is mirrored in your expression, your country man will call you beautiful and mean every word.

If you had a chance to ask country men what they're looking for in a woman, I think you might be surprised by their answers. Since that's easier for me than you, I cornered three—Carl, Matt, and J.D. I found it interesting that not one said "five foot two, blond, and blue eyes." J.D. is a machinist and lives in town. He did say he likes his women pretty, but when I asked for specifics, he said, "You know, a nice smile. Pretty eyes." He's the quiet type and wants to feel comfortable with a woman.

J.D. did bring up something worth mentioning—whether a city woman would be interested in him at all or consider him too much a "country bumpkin" for her sophisticated city tastes. Remember, you want to be perceived as *approachable.* You won't impress a country man with talk of luxury vacations, cars, or private schools for your children. After all, country kids have that small-classroom, one-on-one attention at their local school!

You will impress country men by being yourself and taking an interest in what they have to say.

Matt owns a large ranch. He's interested in a helpmate, a woman both smart and capable. He's attracted to women who are passionate about something that they're involved in. "I don't care if it's restoring furniture, saving the environment, or planting a good vegetable garden. I want a woman who's involved in some larger picture, something she can talk to me about." For Matt, caring and commitment are important.

Carl's divorced (yes, it does happen in the country, but when it does, the men usually remarry). He has a small farm, and his two children spend weekends with him. Carl loves kids and mentioned he wouldn't mind a couple more. He also likes women who have a nice laugh and a sense of humor. "I'm looking for a woman who'll listen after a hard day. Somebody I care about and want to come home to." Then he smiled and added, "I wouldn't mind a good cook, either. And someone who'd pretty up the place."

Like most country women, you'll probably spend a lot of time outdoors working with your man. You might even want to take an active part in ranch life and run a few head of cattle or horses of your own.

Being physically fit is a good idea, no matter where you live. That doesn't mean going to the gym to work out—that's something you'll never have to do again! The country way of life burns calories, whether it's working inside or out or simply walking the back roads with your man. Doesn't that sound better than being stuck indoors on a treadmill headed nowhere?

Chapter 10

What If You're Shy? (How to Make First Contact)

Now let's get down to business—let's talk about how to strike up a conversation with a prospective country beau. You've done your research, chosen a country town, and learned a little about the area. Now's the time to put your plan into action. Heart in hand, you're in town for the day, and ready for the next step. The problem is, you're shy and aren't quite sure how to approach people.

I suggest you start with a leisurely stroll down Main Street. Just for fun, let's say you spot an interesting-looking guy you'd like to meet. You're the shy type and wouldn't have the first idea of how to talk to him first. You get heart palpitations just thinking of how to get his attention. What do you do?

First of all, relax. Take a deep breath, let it out, and smile.

Country folk smile and nod slightly at everybody they see. It doesn't matter if you know each other or not. That's probably the easiest way to let people know you're nice and friendly. Isn't that how you'd react if you saw a cute little six-year-old coming your way? Wouldn't you smile? That's exactly what one woman I know did when a red-haired, freckle-faced kid ran toward her. Of course, Janet also saw a tall, handsome man in jeans and a cowboy hat sauntering along behind him, one eye on the kid and the other on her. When they made eye contact, Janet blushed, but she noticed the cowboy smiled at her.

She didn't know what to do next, but when the cowboy came closer, he touched the brim of his hat, said, "Good mornin'," and paused slightly.

That pause gave Janet the courage to speak up, because she saw correctly that the cowboy was as shy as she was, and he'd taken the first step. It was up to her to return the compliment. "Good morning," she said. "Hot today, isn't it?" With the words barely out of her mouth, she decided that was the dumbest thing she could have said. The cowboy's grin only grew wider, he commented that she must not be from around there because it was bound to be hotter next month, then invited her to share a lemonade. A smile simply says you're approachable, not that you're trying to hustle a date.

Hold that smile until he makes eye contact, whether it's three or four seconds or a long ten.

I know I'm asking you to do something that's really hard—to give this man a look of honest interest, not sheer terror, so I'll also give you a tip.

In those few seconds you're looking at each other, imagine yourself strolling hand in hand down a country lane with this man. Imagine how good you'd feel having a handsome, country beau. Imagine that it's *this* man!

That flight of fantasy should lessen your anxiety a bit *and* show on your expression. Just for practice, try smiling and counting in your head. Even five or six seconds is a long time. It can also be an invitation. It's subtle, but you'll get a response. When he smiles back, maintain eye contact. You've just engraved that invitation with his name, signed, sealed, and delivered!

Now, you've got to say something. Voice can be a powerful connection between two people. Think about how voice affects you when you pick up the phone and hear someone you care about say hello. Do you smile and feel happy that they called? Sure you do! That's the feeling you want to give this country man, so say something simple, like "Hi" or "Nice day, isn't it?"

Better yet, ask him a question. Ask about anything.

If you're on Main Street, ask for directions to Second. You can even ask his opinion on something. Where's the best pizza, ice cream, or gift shop? Say something, even if you're embarrassed, or tongue-tied, or feel yourself blush. Those are all traits of a sweet, shy woman, and that's what you are. But remember, this is your chance. You don't want to miss out on a great guy!

If you're at *any* event being held in *any* small community, you don't need a reason to strike up a conversation. Country Ways are naturally friendly. Just give him a gentle smile, introduce yourself, and say you're new to the area (town, event, whatever).

Now he has a reason to ask you a few questions. After all, he's the expert. He's sure to ask about your interest in the area (town, event, whatever), so be sure to have a few answers at hand. Do mention that you're thinking about making a move from city to country. If he thinks you're a tourist, his interest will wane. Country folk lump tourists in one category and country wannabes in another. You want him to know you're in the second group.

If you're *really* shy, you might try using a prop.

Sports team caps and jackets won't work—most country men care more about local teams than national. I've found the best prop to be a dog. Put him on a leash and stroll down Main Street or head for the local Little League game. Cute dogs, big dogs, little dogs—all bring a smile to anybody's face. If Fido wags his tail incessantly or walks up to strangers, all the better. You've got an automatic icebreaker. A dog also lessens your anxiety if you're walking or jogging alone. If you don't own a dog, borrow your next door neighbor's to take along on your country excursion!

Claire, a single friend of mine who lives in a small town, has a dog who's hard to beat—she's a lovable Irish wolfhound named Dove. Claire's five feet one, and Dove is *huge,* with a bounce to her step and a perpetual grin. Men are fascinated by this dynamic duo and don't hesitate to ask Claire about her four-legged companion. Anyway, that's the reason they give for stopping to talk to her. The point is, the prop is a point of reference; it gives you something to talk about without holding yourself out for rejection. Who wants to do that? On the other hand, you do want to meet that special guy. That means taking risks with your feelings.

The only comfort I can offer is that men risk rejection more than we do. The more you can lower their anxiety level, the better. The more approachable you seem, the better. After all, what's a shy country man to do? He sees you, thinks you're pretty, but he's tongue-tied. Somebody's got to make the first move. Let it be you! Ask for directions, say "Good afternoon" in your friendliest voice, or just smile. Remember, if you see that stranger across a crowded room or fall in love at a glance, don't let that opportunity slide by. Take a chance, and odds are you'll be glad you did!

CHAPTER 11

How to Tell If He's Single

You can tell he's single by looking for a ring, right? Wrong! If a man wears a band of gold, you can pretty well assume he's married, but the *absence* of one does not mean he's single. Many country men don't wear jewelry of any kind for safety reasons. When you work with machinery, construction materials, tools, and equipment, there's a real hazard to wearing jewelry. Cowboys and ranchers run the same risk in working with ropes and leather straps. If that ring gets caught, you could lose a finger, or worse.

The real answer is that you can't tell at first glance if a country guy is available, and maybe that's just as well. I say that because you should be looking for friends as well as a possible love match. Since I recommend marrying your best friend anyway, that's a good place to start.

Part of your game plan should be to be friendly to every man you meet, no matter his age or circumstance.

Old men, young men, and every age in between. Doctor, lawyer, cowboy or farmer. I'm not recommending outrageous flirting or anything that could be misinterpreted, but everyone likes a little attention now and then. Men are no exception.

I also suggest not being any friendlier to a man you *hope* is available than you would to a nice guy who happens to be married.

Adhere to this rule of thumb, and you'll never fall into the trap of being so flirtatious that you seem desperate—a real turnoff to any man. Besides, you never know who might be standing on the other side of the room, watching. If he's married, it could be his wife! You don't want to be *wrongly* perceived as coming on to somebody's husband, and you definitely want to be her friend. Why? If you've been reading carefully, you know the answer—because she knows who *is* available, and if she likes you, she'll want to introduce you. Maybe his mother, sister, or aunt is standing close by. Maybe they're forming an opinion of you right now!

One clue to a man's marital status may be if you repeatedly see him *only* in the company of other men.

People with things in common do tend to group together, and that sometimes includes single men and women. How do you feel about approaching a man who's got three buddies standing with him? No, I didn't think you'd be comfortable doing that. So, a word to the wise. Don't put yourself in that situation, either. You want to be approachable, and if a guy thinks he'll have to "run the gauntlet" to talk to you, he may shy away.

Another way to find out if a man is available is to ask a woman you've met or someone you might feel comfortable introducing yourself to.

Remember, country women are your best allies. Not only will she know if a man is eligible, she might tell you all about him. Do take that information with a grain of salt. After all, it's always possible he dated her best friend for a few months, and although he wanted to call things off, the friend felt differently. Agendas aren't always on the table, and you don't want to assume everyone has a clear picture of the situation.

If you're having a conversation with a man, he won't have any particular reason to tell you if he's married or seeing someone. After all, Country Ways does mean having a friendly attitude toward everybody. Just because he isn't interested in you *romantically* doesn't mean he wouldn't like to get to know you better. Remember, it's perfectly acceptable to have male friends.

It shouldn't be necessary to mention this, because you've heard it from everyone you know (including your mother) and even people you don't know, but here goes.

Under no circumstances should you become romantically involved with a man who's married or in a committed relationship.

Your reputation will be trashed, and in most cases you'll end up unhappy and alone. Country Ways are pretty traditional, and memories are long. Women won't trust you, and men may think you're *easy.* This is a lethal combination for City *or* Country Ways. Besides, why would you want to date somebody else's husband or lover? There are plenty of eligible men in the country, and you only have to find *one.* Since you're reading this book (and I'm writing it) to show you how to reach your goal, you're well on your way toward success. Just keep taking small bites and chewing real hard and you'll get what you want—your very own slice of country heaven!

SECTION TWO

Relationships—Country Style

CHAPTER 12

Messages from the Heart

How do you know if a country man is interested? Will he take the lead? How will he respond if you pursue him? Should you give him your work or home number, or not at all? If he doesn't call, what do you do when you see him in town? How can a chance meeting with his friends give you important clues about your relationship? Will you understand the signs, or does this *country* thing mean you're lost in the woods with no help in sight?

Country Ways *are* different, and you do need to be familiar with the country approach to communication. Understanding your man, and helping him understand you, are key elements to any successful relationship. Country men are gentlemen—born and bred. That *can* be confusing, since compared with no-

nonsense city talk, country can sound downright *courtly.* It's important to distinguish correctly between messages from a man's heart, country manners, and flights of fancy. You don't want to send the wrong signals, either, so let's tackle both these issues.

How do you know if a country man is interested?

The easy answer is that it all starts with a smile—both yours *and* his. Sometimes the first step is more subtle. It's a glance out of the corner of his eye or a quick turn of the head when he first sees you. Making eye contact tells him you're interested. A smile, whether shy or bold, confirms that interest.

Will he take the lead?

Most country men will make the first move, asking for your phone number or an evening's companionship. If you let a country man know you'll be in town only on weekends, you may receive an on-the-spot invitation. How you handle that depends on the situation. You don't want to appear too eager, but if the invitation fits into the day (you're at the rodeo, it's almost dinnertime, and he invites you to the on-site evening barbecue), by all means accept!

This is your chance to hear all about his life. Men like to talk about themselves, so listen and ask questions. Learn all you can about the town, his farm, ranch, or business, what crops or animals he raises—anything at all. Ask his advice on everything from how to start your own country-based business to which vegetables grow best in his garden.

Keep in mind that your schedule is more flexible than his any day of the week. Mother Nature doesn't know the difference between Saturday and Wednesday, and country folk work every day. City dating rules just don't apply out in the Wild West (South, East, North, Heartland *or* the Panhandle). It's hard to let go of what you understand and embrace something new, but your country life depends on it. Don't be disappointed if he thinks Tuesday night is the best night for romance (which could play havoc with *your* schedule) or that he starts yawning at ten because he has to be up at five. Spending time together is just as good in the afternoon as at night or on Thursday instead of Saturday. As long as you both understand that flexibility is a critical part of making your relationship a reality, you'll work things out.

How will he respond if you pursue him?

That all depends on how you handle the pursuit. You don't lose points (or your man) for making the first move, assuming you use subtlety and charm. Some women are comfortable asking men out, some aren't.

Molly, a city woman in her thirties, attended the country rodeo with two girlfriends last year. We ran into each other in the horse barn and were talking when Molly spied a good-looking cowboy standing in a horse stall, currying a palomino. Her girlfriends dared her to go over, and she did, striking up a conversation by asking about the cowboy's horse. Jim seemed very friendly, but he had a legitimate distraction—he had to get ready for a competition.

Molly sent her girlfriends off to the rodeo and stayed behind in the barn to watch the judging. She had a perfect opportunity to talk to Jim after he won a blue ribbon—after all, congratulations were in order. A few minutes into their conversation, a man wanted to talk about a horse Jim had for sale. Molly knew business came first, so she wrote her home number on a piece of paper, slipped it to Jim, and said, "You're busy, and I better catch up with my friends. Call me." He did, later that week.

After they'd been seeing each other for a few months, Jim told Molly he'd been intrigued when she'd given him her number. Jim was looking for a helpmate, someone capable and self-confident in her own right who would understand how important his business was to him. He found his perfect match in Molly.

Should you give him your work or home number, or not at all?

If you decide to give him your telephone number, make it home only. From a country guy's point of view, dealing with receptionists and secretaries doesn't lend itself to romance. It *is* acceptable to take his number and not give him yours. However, this *does* put you in the driver's seat. If that's your style, fine. If not, let him take the lead.

Don't be disappointed if he calls but doesn't ask you out. This is *not* disinterest. He may want to know if you're going to be in town *before* going out on a limb.

He may need to see you on his turf a time or two before asking you out. By all means let him know you're glad he called, whatever the reason. That's only being polite. Give the guy a break—didn't you feel good knowing he wanted to talk to you? If he's a good guy (and he is or you wouldn't have given him your phone number), he deserves to know his feelings are returned. Country men also understand the word "no." If he leaves you a message and you don't return the call, he'll assume you aren't interested.

If he doesn't call, what do you do when you see him in town?

Be cordial and friendly, but don't flirt. He's probably saying no, or at least not for now. Who knows what's going on in his life? Do maintain a courteous, friendly relationship with him. Remember, you will continue to see him around town. You don't want to alienate anybody.

How can a chance meeting with his friends give you important clues about your relationship?

In a small town, you run into people you know—both friends and business acquaintances. Even a drive in the country may result in an unexpected meeting. If someone he knows drives by, don't be surprised if your country man (or the other driver) pulls over to the side of the road for a talk. When this kind of chance encounter arises, your beau should want to introduce you. Not only is he being polite, he's showing the other person (and you) that you're part of his life. Remember, actions *do* speak louder than words.

If you're together, and people come up to say hello, that's partly because they want to know who you are. Watch them for clues. Are they smiling? Eager to meet you? Do women ask where you're from and if you have children? Do they invite *both* of you to their house for dinner or mention there's a dance next Saturday night? This is a good sign! This means your man probably hasn't had a relationship in some time, and they're hoping you're *the one.* If he's seeing a different woman every few months, his women friends will be cordial, but they probably won't invite you to dinner.

Will you understand the signs, or does this country *thing mean you're lost in the woods with no help in sight?*

Country Ways will help you reach your goal if you chart a map, pay attention to the road signs, and be on the lookout for your best friend—country style. Treat men with respect and kindness, and that's what you'll get in return. Treat them like puppies-in-training and you're likely to get growled at—or worse. Men are not the enemy, and they're not pawns in a game. Country men are for real, and they're looking for real women in return. Pay attention, ask questions, and listen, and you'll be just fine.

The paradox to being open and honest is that sometimes a man's interest is heightened if a woman seems somewhat unattainable. So how do you handle the fact that you've already told him you want to move to the country? Doesn't that mean he'll take you for granted or, worse yet, think you need him more than he needs you? No, not if you turn the situation to your advantage. Let him know you are looking at several towns—and at this point you should be. Every man likes a challenge, and he'll step right up to convince you that his town is the best. After all, he lives here!

The distance factor between city and country will create some problems, but do *not* give in to the urge to drive two hours to see him on an evening when you're bored or lonely.

Country men work hard. They put in long days and are usually in bed by ten or eleven. Besides, you should be busy. You want him to feel that he'd be lucky to snatch you up before some other guy finds you. You might consider alternating weekends for a couple of months, too. See him one weekend and go it alone the next. Remember, once you're *keeping company*, you've pretty much given up the option of seeing another man.

Make sure your life is full of interesting things to do, and I'd advise against whining about problems at work.

Remember, country men are problem solvers, and unless you're ready to listen to his advice, don't complain. Save that for girlfriends or your mother. He already thinks your commute is hell on wheels and can't understand why you would endure it. Why give him an opportunity to remind you?

When I was writing to my country man, I filled the pages with cheerful accounts of both work and play. My life was full. I was happy. He wrote more often. He pursued. I went on with my life and wrote back. He pursued harder. I doubted. He pursued harder. I doubted some more. Eventually he won the battle and achieved his goal—me! The best part is that I got what I wanted, too—my best friend, lover, life partner, and country living, all in one fell swoop.

CHAPTER 13

Romance First, Sex Later—Much Later

It's generally true that men want sex earlier in a relationship than women. It's also true that men expect women to set the rules for sexual intimacy. What's proper, and what's not, have run the gamut between the chaste morals of the fifties, the swinging seventies, and the AIDS- and STD-aware nineties.

The man usually makes the first move. You encourage or discourage based on the social mores of the time. Now that we have readily available sources for protection from sexually transmitted diseases and birth control, the situation is both easier and much harder.

Women sometimes feel they need an *excuse* to say no, and here it is: You want the forever kind of love, a relationship headed toward a partnership or marriage. If that's what you're looking for, sexual compatibility is important, but it isn't your number one priority. Sure, you could have a great time with a good-looking, irresponsible guy who's short on potential and long on charm. But once you're out of bed, he won't hold your interest. You're too smart to forge a *bond* with this man. You've set your sights a lot higher than that. You're looking for a relationship that will allow you to live Country Ways!

So, first things first.

Your goal is to find a man who's strong, capable, and intelligent. A man who shares your interests, has a warm smile, a twinkle in his eye, and a good heart. Find a man you're attracted to for all the right reasons.

That's why sex should be further down on your list of priorities—because without all those other attributes, sexual compatibility doesn't matter a whole lot. If you just want to have a good time, that's another story—and another book. Country Ways is about knowing what's best for you, going after it, and being willing to wait for what you want. Intimacy is special. Why turn romance and courtship into something ordinary? Waiting will only whet your appetite. Longing will make it all the more memorable. We all put a higher value on things worth waiting for, things that have a *cost* associated with them. I'm not talking dollars and cents—I'm talking an investment of time, energy, and emotion.

This is not always easy. Putting off sex with someone

you're attracted to can be very difficult. Although it's certainly possible to start a committed relationship by having sex on the first or second date, the odds are against it. Country Ways makes your chances even more difficult. In a small town everybody knows whom you're seeing, now and last year, too. If you want a committed relationship or marriage, you can't carve too many notches on your bedpost.

- On the first date, kissing is about as far as you should allow things to go. Even if you've spent time with him at community events and feel you're ready to take the next step toward intimacy—don't.

Kissing can be *very* intimate. Enjoy it, but remember it's up to you to keep things under control. Your country man knows it's your call to decide when to become physically intimate. It's all right for a man to want *more.* You probably do, too. But if he pressures you, tell him to take a hike. If he isn't willing to give you the time you need, he isn't interested in pursuing a love match. Do your best to keep him as a friend, at least for now. You *will* see him again.

- Keep your conversation light. No double entendres with undertones of sexual meaning, no steamy comments or suggestive banter.

You don't want him to think you'd welcome anything more than kissing. Most men need only a *little* encouragement to make a pass, and you don't want any misunderstandings. Flirting is fun, but draw the line on the safe side. Being a tease can get you attention, but it won't get you a commitment. If he calls you old-fashioned, just smile sweetly and agree!

Country men don't want a woman who's easily talked into sex or anything else.

Real men want a challenge. He might not want to hear "no," but you *will* hold his attention. Waiting will only heighten his desire (and yours). By the time you become sexually intimate, you should care about each other and have shared a laugh or two. Sex doesn't have to be serious. Of course, you should use the same precautions you would with any other man—safe sex is the only sex worth having. But by all means, have a good time! Show him you want him as much as he wants you. Men love women who are not only willing, but eager and responsive.

One of the nicest things you can do for a man is to let him know you enjoy having sex with him.

I do *not* mean batting your eyelashes and saying, "It was good for me, was it good for you?" A few satisfied sighs and a gentle touch on his thigh or shoulder will do nicely.

This also brings up the issue of what you find exciting and what excites him. This is always tricky, and I'd suggest adopting "slow and honest" as your motto. The first few times you make love, take your time getting to know him intimately. Remember, we're going over new ground here. Whispering that something feels good is a better way to get your point across than giving him instructions. Be gentle. Men are more vulnerable than women when it comes to sex. They can't fake arousal. Don't talk about previous sex partners or ask him about the last woman he dated. Just enjoy learning about him and his body and helping him learn *your* most sensitive pleasure spots. Country men like to please their women. Don't make the mistake of thinking country men are sexually inexperienced or dull. Quite the contrary! You just may learn a thing or two from your backwoods beau. Personally, I find it intriguing that a man who's good with his hands is *good with his hands!*

How should you behave the next morning? Well, country men are different from city types, but not *that* different. Just because you've become sexually intimate doesn't mean you should be making plans to pack up and move in. You might share a leisurely breakfast and make plans for the rest of the day, but he might have to get up early to feed the livestock or go to work. Don't cling to him or act insecure, even though you might feel it—especially if your thoughts are on commitment and marriage and he jumps out of bed and goes to work, just as though it's any other morning. Instead, take a deep breath, get dressed, and go about your day. By all means smile and be friendly, but remember, although the relationship *has* taken a giant step, there's a lot more to come.

If, after a few months, you decide he isn't the one, it's important to take your time before starting to see another country man.

- *Do* come to town alone, and *do* make it known that you're no longer seeing what's-his-name.

- *Don't* talk about him or what went wrong.

Remember, he lives here. You will see him again. Besides, you could be talking to his cousin or someone who went to grade school with him. People in small towns tend to know everybody, and there's nothing wrong with letting people know you're no longer seeing him—in fact, that's a good idea. Another country beau is probably waiting in the wings. But remember, it's not just gentlemen who don't kiss and tell. Be a lady tonight and every night!

CHAPTER 14

Ladies and Gentlemen

Country Ways lean toward the traditional, and whether it's your first time out together or your tenth, that includes letting him pay the bill. It doesn't matter if it's an expensive night out or a simple drive in the country, don't offer to split expenses. You may not know if he has money to burn or is on a tight budget, but that's not the issue. Don't make any assumptions about his financial status, simply *assume he knows what he's doing*. That means sitting back and letting him take charge.

The fact that you may not fit the mold of a traditional woman may be one reason he's attracted to you. Sound like a contradiction in terms? Maybe so, but putting a little country in a city woman can be quite a challenge, and what strong man doesn't like a challenge? On the other hand, I don't recommend making it any harder than it has to be. Do you want him to think you can do perfectly well without him? Of course not! You know you can pay your own way; there's no reason to make a point of your independence.

You can learn a lot about your man by watching how he conducts himself in the beginning of your relationship.

It will make him happy to find things that please you, including footing the bill for the pleasure of your company. It makes a man feel good to arrange an evening with his girl and have her enjoy both his company and his plans. Don't take that away from him. Encourage him to do it again!

In return, be *courteous*. Take the time to appreciate him, listen to what he has to say, and ask a few questions that show you're interested in *him*.

Your reaction to *him* is of prime importance. He both wants and needs your approval, trust, and admiration. Sending a handwritten note on pretty stationery is an especially nice way to say thank you. So is a smile that makes him feel he's special. It's magic when a man does little things for his woman. How you respond has a lot to do with how much attention you'll get later on. With a little effort you can make him feel loved—so much so that he'll keep up the good work!

If he *isn't* doing little things for you, it might be because you're so self-sufficient. Although this is good for the long haul, if you want him to feel chivalrous, he needs to be able to do things for you. If you smoke, don't dig in your purse for a lighter. Smile sweetly and wait half a minute. He'll enjoy lighting your cigarette for you. Don't rush to get out of the car. Give him time to walk around and open your door. Don't act surprised when he pulls out the chair for you at dinner. Instead, smile and say "Thank you." Don't take the gentleman out of your country man. Put the *lady* in you!

Help him out by dropping clues about the kinds of little things you like.

You may think he should know what you want, but he'd much rather know than guess. If you love flowers, admire meadows of wildflowers and front-yard gardens. Mention casually how much a vase of fresh posies lifts your spirits. Order dessert and rave about the creamy texture of imported chocolate. If he suggests Italian and you prefer Chinese, mention you've been craving egg rolls or hot-and-spicy. Give him a chance to please you.

You can either be clear and concise or hint and coax—whichever works best for you. Just be sure to point him in the right direction. Most men are all thumbs when it comes to feminine nature. Country men are no exception. Surprises are sweet, but they're no more important than something he took time to plan. What's important is that he was thinking of you. Give him an opportunity to rescue you from marauding bandits! Let him whisk you onto his horse and ride off into the sunset!

Let him know you value him, say "Please" and "Thank you," and show your delight with his plans for the evening—no matter what he wants to do (within reason, of course).

Personally, I draw the line at destruction derbies. Show me a cattle roundup or an auction and I'm in heaven, but watching cars drive around in circles and crashing into each other is more than I can bear. Remember, you're trying to decide whether or not you want to *keep company* (see chapter 15) with this man. You want to spend time with him and learn all about him. It's important that he learn about you, too. Be up front with your needs and wants, likes and dislikes.

After you've spent time together and been seen around town as a couple, you've probably decided the relationship has possibilities. At this point, townsfolk will assume you're *keeping company.* It's time to move the relationship along. If he invites you for a drive in the country, offer to fix a picnic basket. He may still want to take you out to lunch, but your willingness to contribute to the day is important.

You will earn your man's love and respect by being supportive and nonjudgmental.

If your man does something to annoy you, remember that everybody makes a mistake now and then—even you. While you probably berated yourself at the time, if your man pointed your mistake out to you, would that have helped? I didn't think so. It would have only made you feel worse. A man wants a woman who's positive, not a nag. Don't make him feel he isn't living up to your standards. Don't make a big deal out of whatever it is he's done, even if you decide to break off the relationship. In that case, just let him know things haven't worked out and show up in town *alone* the very next weekend.

Country men work hard because it makes them feel good to take care of their family. *You* are at the core of what family means to a country man. He's been looking for you his entire life. Your enthusiasm, support, and love are central to his success. That, in turn, goes a long way toward keeping *you* happy. But before we get ahead of ourselves and have you walking down the aisle, let's talk about taking the next step—*keeping company* with your country beau.

CHAPTER 15

Country Men Don't Date—They Keep Company

Country Ways are significantly different from city customs, and that includes the concept of dating. For the most part, dating is like being on stage. A situation (for example, a date) is created and played out, which may have little to do with everyday life. Dating can be fun and exciting, but sometimes it's only an illusion. Dating may be a good start, but if your goal is marriage, I don't think you should play the dating game with any man for very long. Give it some time, of course, but at some point you have to make a "call." If you aren't *both* interested in taking the relationship a step further, it's time to move on.

Life is a timed event, and if you're going to attain your goals, you've got to get on with it. Frankly, I think dating is nothing more than a playground for people either unable or unwilling to make a commitment. That's *not* what life, or Country Ways, is about.

Keeping company is an expression of how a couple spends authentic, quality time together. It's understanding that getting to know each other, and doing ordinary, day-to-day things together, is more important than where you go. It's the point in a relationship where a couple is trying things on for size to see whether or not they're going to fit. It's when you're *both* considering the possibility of a long-term, committed relationship, forging a life together, and creating your version of family, home, and forever. Keeping company is real life, played in real time, and that means getting serious.

Don't misunderstand my philosophy on dating—I'm *not* saying that once you start keeping company you won't go out anymore. That's something you should do for the rest of your life together. But remember, when you go to that local restaurant or theater, chances are your country man will know half the people there. You won't have him to yourself, and he won't be able to focus his time and attention on just you. Country folk are friendly, and everybody knows just about everybody in a small town. His favorite restaurant will be full of people he knows. News travels fast, and word will get out that you're seeing each other. Believe me, this will be a major news item. Although there's a positive side to an evening with a "see and be seen" objective, there's also a negative.

Remember your goal and your game plan. You want a marriage or life partner, and you're committed to living in the country. It's important to have quality time with this man. You're going to decide whether or not you want to play for keeps. Instead of the old routine, how about trying something new? Haven't you already been out to dinner or the theater more times than you can count?

- Why not ask him to show you the local sights—from his perspective.

You'll get an idea of his interests and be better able to decide whether your lives will mesh comfortably. You may find you have a lot in common and want to start down that discovery road with engines roaring. On the other hand, if he goes game hunting every weekend and you're a vegetarian, you may want to look for someone else.

- By focusing on activities that teach you something about him, you'll be better able to decide whether you want to keep company.

If you discover genuine common ground and shared interests, you're that much ahead. If he introduces you to new opportunities and activities that pique your curiosity, that's terrific!

- It's also important to let him know what kinds of things you like to do.

You're looking for a balanced relationship, and if he's your kind of guy, he'll want to know all about you and anything that interests you. If not, you may want to think about moving the relationship from love interest to friendship. Be careful and don't hurt his feelings, but be realistic—you don't want to invest time in a relationship that's headed down a one-way street. Unfortunately, you can't continue to see him while looking for someone else. In the country, if you're going to be taken seriously, you can keep company with only one man at a time. Country Ways are old-fashioned, and country men don't want a "fast" woman.

Monogamy is *in* and promiscuity *out.* You can't change partners very often—two or three a year at most.

That's why it's a good idea to get to know each other at community events *before* spending time alone. You'll already be past the initial "we're attracted to each other" phase and in the "this relationship has possibilities" phase. Although the first part can be carried out in public, the second definitely requires a one-on-one component.

Where you go together is less important than how the relationship progresses.

If romance is in bloom, those first times together will be the cornerstone to how you spend the rest of your lives. You'll reach back into those memories over the years to recapture the way you felt in the beginning. If this is *your* country guy, you're building a foundation to last a lifetime. You need a strong, reality-based foundation, not a fancy, souped-up model that goes out of style in a year or two. It doesn't matter what you do, or how you do it, as long as you're headed down the same road. I've heard that being in love means you're looking in the same direction. That means sharing the same interests, goals, hopes, and dreams.

You should both be open to new ideas and things to see and do together.

Find what you have in common and what you can build on for the future. Give yourself time to discover that about yourselves. Have some fun, too! Remember, there's a fine balance between being open to new ideas and adopting his interests just to please him. That's something you *don't* want to do, because it will just come back to haunt you. Country Ways isn't about pretense; it's about sharing genuine, common ground.

Attending a talk entitled "The Endangered Western Snowy Plover" can move your romance along better than going to the movies, and talking about cattle ranching, repairs to the barn, or raising prize-winning vegetables can bring you closer than asking him to take you *anywhere.* Why? Because the cinema is a few hours of fun (which is okay), but nature and the environment are part of his everyday world. That's where you want to be. You're not looking for a Friday night date, you're interested in forever.

I met my country man at a seaside conference near Monterey, California. We spent a lot of time talking about small-town life, ranching, and permaculture (forms of agriculture that allow the land to produce in perpetuity). What started out as mutual interest quickly flamed into what was to become a great love affair through a fairly unusual medium—the U.S. mail. Our letter writing grew quickly from once a week to a daily expression of shared interests and passion that transcended a thousand-mile distance. Sound romantic? It was. I occasionally go back and reread those letters and marvel at how a chance meeting changed my life so dramatically.

After two months of reading and writing, I knew we'd passed through phase one and were in the throes of phase two. It was time to fly north for a visit. After my guy retrieved me from the airport with a *very* welcoming kiss, we stopped off at the hardware store. Yes, the hardware store. It may sound corny, but seven years later we still talk about how we walked the aisles of the hardware store hand in hand. That simple beginning was the start to a passionate weekend that eventually brought me love, my lifelong best friend, and Country Ways.

One of the allures of a country romance is the discovery that you don't need five-star restaurants, snooty maître d's, or Broadway shows for romance to bloom. In fact, you might find what you're looking for in places you'd *never* have thought to look. Personally, I now find hardware stores *very* romantic!

Chapter 16

Be His Best Friend

Mata Hari was mysterious, Greta Garbo soul stirring, and Madonna scandalous. Unless you're a movie star or the sultry goddess type, you have a better shot at being his *best friend.* Leave the role-playing to women who aren't smart enough to know mystery and fantasy are a sometime thing. You're looking for a lifelong relationship. That starts with being the woman you want him to fall in love with—yourself. Anything else is just "smoke and mirrors," and you're not an illusion: you're the real thing! Whether you're interesting, outgoing, and a lot of fun or quiet, shy, and downright sweet, it makes no difference—there's a country man just for you.

I'm a firm believer in honesty. I don't have the time, energy, or interest to maintain a fantasy life.

Even if I did, I wouldn't. I'm in this relationship for the long haul, and it has to work for the *real* me. I know you feel the same.

Best friends aren't mysterious, and they don't keep secrets.

They *tell* secrets—to each other! Everyday life is the stuff of dreams. The Emerald City may have been exciting, but it wasn't long before Dorothy wanted to get back to Kansas. If you've always had female best friends, it may seem odd to think of your man in that role. I know I felt that way. I'd never confided my *true* feelings to a man, not the ones you whisper over the phone to girlfriends. I couldn't risk it. What if he laughed at my insecurities? Rolled his eyes when I told him how I really felt? Let me tell you, I had a lot to learn, and am I glad I did! Give up your stereotypes, ladies. Work on being best friends with your country man. Isn't *he* the one you want to live with? Don't you want to grow old with *him?* Whom better to trust?

There's nothing more passionate than friendship. When you marry your best friend, the talk never dies, the intimacy never stops, the sex never becomes routine. You grow together, love together, and work things out together. Country men are smart—they know best friends stand the test of time. Best friends stick together, forgive your faults, and applaud your achievements. If that sounds more practical than romantic, maybe it is. But those are key ingredients for keeping love alive and maintaining a lifelong commitment.

A word of caution: Be mindful of timing. Being honest doesn't mean you should confide intimate secrets on the first or second date.

I don't see any reason he should know you were fired from your last job, your grandparents were never legally married, or your sister just announced she's dating Ellen DeGeneres. *Some* things are best left in the closet for the moment. Wait until after he kisses you madly (while you hesitantly, and with great reluctance, stop things from going any further). Wait until sparks are blasting like the Fourth of July, and this is definitely going somewhere. Wait until you're keeping company. *Then* tell him those little family secrets! All you need is a little time and tenderness for friendship to blossom into love.

Marriage and life partnerships are serious business, and so are country men. They're looking for women who are both supportive and loving. Someone to dream dreams with and make them come true *together.* They don't want a night out with the boys (although they may want to go hunting or fishing with the guys once in a while). But what if he'd rather take his best friend along?

Why not go with him? Learn a thing or two and have a good time while you're at it!

Independence is good, but I prefer being together. That's one benefit to country living. Whether it's chores, errands, or sharing an interesting article from the newspaper, I like sharing my man's life rather than watching from the sidelines. In the city you hear about what he's been doing more than doing things together. I've found that the talk never grows old if you're walking down memory lane together. Being there with him, being part of his life, is what Country Ways is all about.

One of the things I have in common with my guy is our love of books. It doesn't matter if it's a blockbuster novel, how-to book, or anything in between. I enjoy reading passages to him, knowing he'll be interested, whether it's a romance novel or an essay on economics. He reads to me, too, whether it's alternative energy or pole barn construction. We also sleuth bookstores together, especially the ones that carry used books. We're like little kids, roaming the aisles, happy as clams when we find something particularly offbeat or outlandish. I enjoy tagging along to the lumberyard, and he's my sidekick when I traipse through secondhand shops. Isn't that what best friends do together? Have fun, no matter what your definition of "fun" is!

I think it's important in any relationship to see each other as interesting, intriguing people. The fact that you're even *more* interesting when you're together is icing on the cake. Differences can keep you apart, but they can also bring you together.

Open yourself to the possibility of seeing things in a different light, and you open up a new world of possibilities.

That's what moving to the country is all about, and it should definitely be part of your game plan. This is the stretch of road between the past and the future when memories are made and traditions established. Remember, if you love your best friend, you'll always want to come home to each other. We all know if you can make it with anybody, it's your best friend. Just open yourself up to the idea and you'll do just fine.

CHAPTER 17

Welcome to His World

If you're keeping company, you're taking the relationship to a higher, more important level. In most cases it takes couples a while to get in sync and to smooth their rough edges into a good, solid fit. Because he's country, you'll need more time (and a little help) interpreting his actions than you would with a city guy. Remember, you're maneuvering in new territory and can't expect the road signs to be the same in the country as they are in city traffic.

One of the first bridges to cross is your first visit to his house. When a country man invites you to his home, he's showing you that he's strong, capable, and responsible. He's also demonstrating that he can be a good provider. This is important to him. The fact that he *wants* to show you is a very good sign. Crossing this bridge *carefully* will go a long way toward shaping your future with this man and how you will fit into his life.

Pride, accomplishment, and self-respect: that's how a man feels about the place he's carved out for himself in the country. His feelings for the land never waver, whether it's been a good year or bad. He's watched newborn calves take their first steps and raised wheat to feed them. He's built fences, dug ditches, and drunk water from his own well. He loves every inch of his world, and he wants you to love it, too.

If your country man owns a farm or ranch, it's a good idea to keep a handle on your expectations.

Keep an open mind, and pay close attention. You don't want to be disappointed, and you don't want your country man to be disappointed in your reaction to his beloved property. Remember, the land may have been in his family for generations, or he may have saved for years to build that house.

Be prepared to *not* like what you see and to *not* tell him how you feel.

This is not being dishonest; this is being wise. If you're pleasantly surprised by his house or ranch, so much the better. In the movies and on television, farms and ranches are pristine and picturesque. The house may be painted white, have cutout gingerbread trim and a gabled roof, or be a sprawling log cabin with four bedrooms and three baths. There are flowers growing everywhere. The barn is impressive and newly painted. Beautiful, freshly polished saddles and tack are arranged neatly inside. The cattle and sheep pens are dry, the chickens are all in their coop, and the pigs are freshly scrubbed and a very pretty pink.

Please put that picture out of your mind. This is *not* a working farm or ranch. This is a movie set. Your man's house may need a coat of paint, and the barn may be more functional than picturesque. The garden may be sprouting weeds, and the cattle and sheep pens probably need some attention. The chickens may be running loose, and the pigs are more brown than pink (pigs will be pigs—they like mud and they *do* wallow). Stacks of lumber seem to grow like weeds in the country. One day you have a few, and the next thing you know, there's enough lying around to build a second barn. You may notice a lot of equipment and machinery you'd think should be better stored out of the rain, too. In most cases, barn space is saved for animals, hay, and grain storage, and everything else manages well enough outside.

Disappointed? Do you have an irresistible urge to ask why there's so much *stuff* lying around? Don't!

Do consider a farm or ranch as a work-in-progress and continually under construction.

Your man will always be building or repairing something, and he's always going to be finishing, starting, or in the middle of several projects. Schedules are subject to change owing to acts of nature like the weather, birthing, milking, weaning, planting, and harvesting time (just to name a few). It might be a good idea to adjust your expectations *before* visiting his home. (I wish someone had told me that before I visited my country man's home. I thought those TV shows and movies portrayed *real* life on the range!)

Don't try to judge your man's financial situation by the number of projects he currently has under construction.

He may have money to spend, he may not have ready cash to finish things, or he may just stockpile materials. He may be putting things off because he just bought a tractor, a prize mare, or a champion ram. He may have extra cash because the wheat crop just came in or his best stallion is earning his keep in stud fees. At this point, the best thing you can do is to watch and learn. Given a little time, you'll get a better idea of his financial situation, and that's soon enough.

He won't expect you to be impressed with his house or furnishings because he probably hasn't given them a second thought. You don't want to hurt his feelings, so keep a rein on any *major* disappointment. Instead, consider his home a blank canvas awaiting your personal brush strokes of color and style. Believe me, he won't mind. He's looking forward to those feminine touches because they announce to the world that you're in his life *and* that you're here to stay!

Your "nesting instincts" will make him feel loved because he wants you to make his house *your* home.

He'll probably go along with whatever you want because he wants *you.*

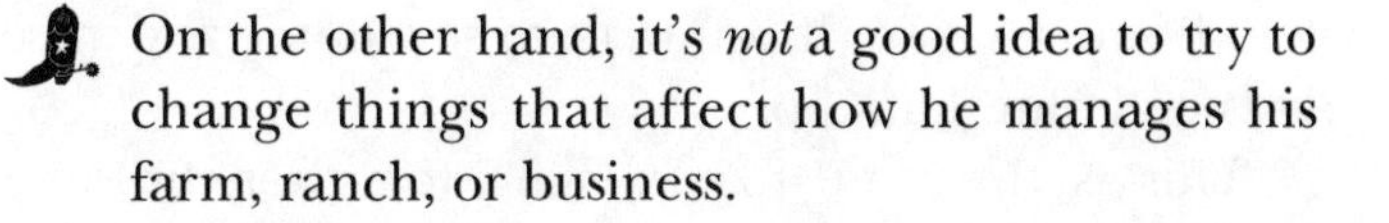

On the other hand, it's *not* a good idea to try to change things that affect how he manages his farm, ranch, or business.

That's clearly his department at this stage of your relationship. Whether this comes into play later will depend on how you intertwine your lives. It takes time to figure out how you'll fit together, and interlocking the pieces of the puzzle is half the fun. You'll find ways to put your individual stamp on his life, and however you do that will please him.

Express an interest in his everyday activities, whether that's his business, cattle ranching, horses, computers, the apple orchard, or cooking vegetables you find growing in the garden.

Bring your paints and easel, hiking boots, binoculars for birdwatching, or laptop computer if you long to write. This is his chance to learn about you, too. As I've mentioned before, show him what interests and delights you.

More important, show him how you might fit in to these new surroundings.

Don't deprive him of seeing you excited about his ranch and the life you can have there with him. This is a chance to make *your* dreams come true, too! He'll want to be part of that process. If you've always wanted to breed and train dogs, tell him. If you dream of a backyard greenhouse and garden full of vegetables and flowers, say so. If you want to stay home and raise kids, tell him that, too.

This is the time for working together, holding hands, dreaming dreams, and falling in love. It's important to know what you're getting from a relationship as well as what you're giving. Talk about these and other issues, because ultimately you're each responsible for your own happiness. That means doing your best to shape this new relationship into a new life. That's an important component to living happily ever after, and with a strong country man by your side, your goal is clearly in sight!

CHAPTER 18

Pickup Trucks, Short Skirts, and Country Music

A month after our first intimate interlude, and while still separated by almost a thousand miles, my country guy and I decided to meet halfway for a romantic weekend. Since I headed to the airport directly from work on Friday, I wore my usual business suit but chose one with sex appeal—the skirt was short and the blouse silk.

I knew he'd be driving four hundred miles, but in my romance-induced fog, I hadn't thought much about the details. Although I was certainly aware my guy was country, it never occurred to me that he would pick me up in a pickup truck. Of course, I knew he had one, I just didn't put two and two together! It was a case of fantasy coming face-to-face with reality. I was dressed in corporate chic, he in jeans, shirt, and boots. It was a nice pair of jeans and a new shirt, but we didn't look like a *couple.* We didn't *look* as though we belonged together.

We walked hand in hand through the airport, the parking lot, and to his truck. I realized I had a big problem when he opened the door and I *climbed* in. The distance from the ground to the truck being somewhat high, my short, straight skirt hiked *way* up. Several times during that evening I flashed as much leg, thigh, and higher as any Las Vegas showgirl. The fact that my country gentleman opened the door for me, and waited for me to get in, meant that he got *quite* an eyeful! Later he told me he'd about blown an eye socket. Did I mention I was wearing nylons and a garter belt?

The point of this story is that our two worlds were on a collision course, and I learned you've got to keep your perspective straight if this adjustment thing is going to work out. Accept that you're not going to see the problems early enough to sidestep them, and neither is he. The best thing you can do is smile, shrug your shoulders, and take things in stride.

Here's one issue that may surprise you, but that you can't sidestep—it's the importance of pickup trucks. Country men *bond* with their trucks. I know you may be rolling your eyes at this, so let me explain. Trucks are to country men what horses are to cowboys. Both get them where they want to go, haul equipment and tools, are dependable, run better for *them* than anyone else, and are an expression of their personality. Your guy will be a Chevy or Ford man—not both. Take note that the hot (and handsome) country singer Alan

Jackson is a television spokesman for Ford. Those commercials are aimed at country as well as "faux" country folk.

A few words to the wise: If a man's truck is an older model, muddy and seen better days, he's a workingman. If his truck is new, shiny, and clean as a whistle, he is *not*. He's either a weekend cowboy or has a town job. Both are perfectly acceptable, but you should know the difference. If your man drives a Chevy, do not praise Fords. If he's a Ford man, the word "Chevy" should not pass your lips! It's possible (but not likely) that you may run into a man who's fond of his Dodge, but very few country men drive the smaller, foreign models.

You'll be a step ahead of the situation if you have a sense of humor. You *are* going to trip over your feet occasionally, and you *are* going to find yourself on unfamiliar ground. Was it better to laugh off my embarrassment at showing too much thigh when climbing into my guy's truck or to be disagreeable because he drives a pickup? My friend Lisa found herself in a similar dilemma the first time she visited her beau's ranch. They were touring the barn when something came up he needed to take care of. Lisa decided to sit on an old overstuffed chair while she waited and quickly discovered a wily chicken had hidden her clutch of eggs in the corner! She laughed it off and spent the next few minutes scrubbing egg from the seat of her pants.

Laughing is good for the human spirit and a sight better than crying. A sense of humor, pickup trucks, and romance bring us to country music. No, I didn't think you'd get that, but give me a minute. You'll catch on. You may not like country music; you may prefer opera, rock and roll, or jazz. That's okay.

Do yourself a favor and give country music a try.

One of the most remarkable things about country men is that they're comfortable with the idea that they *should* have feelings. They think it's cool to be in love, believe in romance, and want to get married. *Good* country music celebrates romance, relationships that stand the test of time, and "the love of a good woman." George Strait has been married for twenty-seven years and makes no bones that he's still crazy about the first woman he ever loved.

My guy usually has the radio on out in his workshop. He's come to the house more than once and dragged me away from my work to hurry back to the shop to listen to a song that reminds him of *us*. Those are the times he pulls me into his arms and thanks me for being in his life. Those are also the times I *truly* know how lucky I am to have found my country man and Country Ways.

The sentiments some men find difficult to express come through loud and clear in the lyrics of a good old country love song. If you're not familiar with this neck of the musical woods, ask your man which are his favorites and buy a CD or two. You may surprise yourself by really taking a shine to the kinds of songs that just may put you and your man in the mood for love! Good music, good companionship—who could ask for more?

CHAPTER 19

Knights in Shining Armor and Their Damsels

Deep inside every country man is a knight in shining armor just waiting for the chance to rescue a damsel in distress or a cowboy hero who'd fearlessly battle outlaws to save the schoolmarm. More than anything, a country man wants to protect, cherish, and serve the woman he loves. He sees himself as noble, sincere, and trustworthy. When you acknowledge these traits in your man, he'll make you the most important person in his life. He'll be loving, generous, caring, and sensitive to your needs.

Country men are a combination of the quintessential alpha male—strong and dominant—and the beta male—compassionate and understanding. In other words, he's the man of your dreams!

Knights and heroes are rewarded with public acclaim, appreciation, and encouragement. When they come home after a long day of slaying ferocious dragons, damsels do not complain, "That dragon is in my way; can't you move it *now*?" When a cowboy hero throws the outlaws in jail, the schoolmarm doesn't snivel, "No muddy boots in the schoolhouse!"

Don't try to improve the way a country man behaves.

You'll only make him feel weak and unloved. A man feels strong when his woman admires and appreciates him. After all, he's country, and that means a wonderful combination of rough edged and tender.

So, how do you treat your country man? The best and simplest answer is, exactly how you'd like him to treat you.

Compliment him whenever possible, and give him positive reinforcement every chance you get. Every time he does something you like, let him know. Tell him you appreciate how handy he is, that he can fix things, works hard, and kisses you first thing in the morning and last thing at night. Admire him when he lifts a hundred-pound bale of hay or takes out the trash. Say "Thank you." Smile. Be happy. This will make him feel loved. Trust me, positive reinforcement works like a charm. I know, because I'm always delighted to be on the receiving end!

Again: Treat him how you'd like to be treated, and you can't go wrong. Do you like to be nagged? How do you feel when somebody is always complaining about how or why you do things? Is that any way to treat someone you care about? No, I don't think so, either. There are many better ways to get a point across, and here's just one example.

My man doesn't pay any attention to what he wears—just grabs the nearest shirt and pair of pants and crawls in. Instead of whining, "Can't you wear something *decent?*" I compliment him when he *does* choose a shirt I particularly like. In no time at all, he's wearing my favorites. Same thing with the trash. Instead of nagging him to take it outside (and getting nowhere), I make a big deal of thanking him when he does remember. After a few weeks, he'll be checking the bin *before* it's full.

Don't act like his mother. Instead be his sweetie and best friend.

My country man and I don't have a set routine of who does what, because neither of us likes "rules." That means we share responsibilities—all of them. Taking out the trash is as much my job as his. So is mucking out the barn and rototilling the garden. I appreciate his doing those things, too! He's also very good at noticing when I do things for him and saying so. Remember, any relationship worth having is good for both you *and* him.

If you want to be treated like a lady, you have to treat him like a gentleman.

Country men like women who are easy to talk to. Acting aloof may give you an appearance of mystery, but a man can't spend his life in mystery—what he wants is acceptance and someone to come home to. Country men marry women who like to laugh, give them a break along the way, and are their best friends. That's the kind of person you can go the distance with. Self-confidence is important, too. You're interesting, accomplished, and a great all-around person. Of course he wants you! Some country men are attracted to strong, independent women; others like their women more on the soft side. *All* country men want a woman with a "stand by your man" attitude. What you get in return is "stand by your woman" respect.

Country men come in all shapes, sizes, and ages, but they do have a few things in common. They're strong, both in mind and body, are committed to family and community, respect tradition and pay their bills on time. They're unfailingly polite and believe children should be, too. Love and marriage are a given to country men, and if divorce does rear its ugly head, they don't give up on love. Given time and the right woman, they'll give it another try. In fact, when a country guy's romancing his best girl under a star-studded sky, settling down *will* be on his mind!

Country men are proud, and there's nothing they like better than bragging about their woman. Whether you're spending time bottle-feeding lambs, working the horses, starting a business, or baking his favorite pie, country men want everyone to know how lucky they are to have you. After all, he gave up his bachelor ways for the only woman capable of changing him! You got what you wanted and pleased him at the same time—that's a win-win situation.

CHAPTER 20

The Way to a Country Man's Heart

Women enjoy receiving romantic gifts. We generally don't like getting toasters or vacuum cleaners for birthdays. Whether he picks a bouquet of wildflowers from his own meadow or buys two dozen roses from a florist, it *is* the thought that counts. When a man takes the time to do something for you that makes you smile, you remember. When he buys you something you especially want, the gift lasts a long time.

Sometimes the least expensive present can mean the most, whether it's a card for no other reason than that he was thinking of you or the magazine my dear heart bought me a few weeks ago. It doesn't matter which magazine it was—Jimmy Smits was on the cover. I sigh over Jimmy Smits, and my guy thinks that's cute!

A few years ago I was researching a Pacific island

atoll as the setting for a historical novel set in the early 1900s. My country man knew almost as much as I did about the island because I'd been talking about the story for months. That Christmas he gave me a wall-size map of the tiny atoll, complete with topography descriptions and fathom sounding readings. I know the map didn't cost much—not in currency. His time and energy are another matter. To me, the map was a gift of love, appreciation, and support for my work.

So if he's doing his best to appreciate you, how do you show your appreciation for him? Let's say you're spending the day together—on his ranch or farm. He's outside working, probably harder than usual because he wants to impress you. His business, the land, and everything on it are an expression of himself—who he is and what he can be. Work is what he does. You need to appreciate, understand, and value this about him.

This may be only the second or third time he's invited you to his house, and although you'll spend some time together, you'll also have time to yourself. You're resourceful. You've either brought work with you, or you'll find plenty to do on your own. How about doing something nice for him? There are plenty of things you can do *with* him, but let's explore the possibility of doing something *for* him.

You might pick a bouquet of flowers for the house, feed the dog, or put groceries away. Those are all nice ideas, but I know something better. Let's talk about cooking. There's no getting around the fact that somebody has to cook. This is the country—pizza parlors don't deliver ten miles from town.

If you want to please a country man, fix dinner.

Use your time and energy to provide him with the strength to work the land (which, in turn, helps him provide for you). Providing nourishment is closely associated with love, and you'll warm his heart with your cooking (as well as his belly). Women are good at connecting with other people. That's the caring and nurturing side of the feminine spirit. When you offer that connection through sustenance, and he starts to *depend* on you for both his physical and spiritual needs, you have connected on a deeper level.

Dependency is *not* a dirty word. Risking reliance on another can lead to the road of self-growth. It's that connection that will make the sum of the two of you more than your separate selves. Depend on each other, trust in yourselves and your relationship, and you will grow together. Growth requires change. In order to change, you must take risks. Risking your feelings can be scary. At some point in the keeping company stage of your relationship, you have to decide whether you can jump and whether your man will be there to catch you. Love is, after all, a leap of faith. Feelings are difficult to talk about because we don't think anyone truly understands exactly how we feel. You'll never know unless you *share* those emotions. That takes trust. Trust begins with making connections. Connections start with depending on each other. Start small. Cook dinner.

If your man is anything like mine, he'll eat about anything you put in front of him and praise you to the skies! Most country men are regular, down-to-earth guys. They like meat, potatoes, and vegetables. Men who work hard need protein, carbohydrates, and large portions. I've never met a country man who doesn't love biscuits and gravy, but tofu is generally *not* a good idea. If you know how to cook great vegetarian dishes, by all means do so. My friend Vicki makes a delicious eggplant lasagna that tastes just like beef, and her husband loves it. If you lean toward gourmet cooking, that's fine, too. Your country man may seem hesitant, but maybe he's never had a chance to try Thai or Ukrainian food. Remember, though, if you don't have a knack for it yet, save these "riskier dishes" till you feel more confident. It may be harder to coax him to like something new when you're not sure of it yourself. But you may be surprised—he may discover a love for French cuisine when you make something "*très* elegant" and special just for him. Believe me, your man will appreciate every little thing you do in the kitchen, whether it's simple Betty Crocker or elaborate Julia Child. Don't be surprised if he wants to tie on an apron and give you a hand. Lots of country men like to cook!

The first time you fix dinner, be sure to check the garden for fresh vegetables.

Look for cherry tomatoes and snap beans tasting like summer and sun, or the sweetest corn imaginable. Did you know the sugar content in corn starts decreasing as soon as it's picked? You can raid his cupboards for everything else you need. Don't expect much. Remember, he's not a gourmet. Whatever you come up with, he's sure to be impressed with your flair for the unusual as well as your ability to cope under pressure.

Don't be shy about giving him a list of things to buy at the store.

He'll think you're wonderful for thinking of him, and you are! When my man goes to the hardware store, his next stop is for groceries. It's important to make his job as easy as possible—after all, you want him to succeed.

I'm careful to make a list, including brand names, sizes of cans or jars, or how many pounds of whatever.

He also stops by a local produce farmer who specializes in unusual baby vegetables and edible flowers. My friend Cindy introduced us to edible flowers with her mint jelly, complete with tiny pink flowers with "explosions" of taste. My guy loves the idea so much, we're planning to add a new section to the garden next spring.

It's important that you not get the wrong impression. I'm not saying you have to become a homemaker if you're more the business or outdoors type. But if you're looking for ways to make him feel special, cooking is a great place to start!

CHAPTER 21

Country Men May Have Rough Edges, but They Aren't "Fixer-Uppers"

You've rented a house with an option to buy. You love the main structure, but you can't wait to get your hands on the inside. You want new carpeting, lighting, and brass fixtures on every door. The outdated wallpaper *has* to go! You're sure that painting the entire house antique ivory will make *such* a difference. And it will. But there's a problem. He may like everything just as it is. This is when you take a deep breath, calm down, and consider your options. The secret to not choking on real life is to take small bites and chew real hard. Neither your country man nor the house needs to be gutted. All they need are some tender loving care and perhaps a little mending.

The biggest complaint men have about women is that they try to change them. If you've found the perfect country man, except for a couple of little things you wish were different, what do you do?

- First, do your best to accept him just as he is, imperfections included.

- Second, choose your battles.

Decide what's really important to your life and your relationship and what boils down to small potatoes. Learn to live with his favorite, grungy shirt and leaving the newspaper on the floor. My guess is you only want to fluff up his rough edges a bit. Maybe convince him to wear a dress shirt on Saturday night or something other than Levi's and boots. Forget it! Why fight a losing battle? And how bad is it, really, to see him wearing what he feels comfortable in? My experience tells me people don't change much anyway. Why drive yourself crazy?

- Do talk to him about things that are integral to your relationship and happiness—whatever those things are.

Save your battles for important issues. Nitpicking and nagging only drain a relationship of love and vitality. Do not assume the role of wise, cultured woman showing your redneck country guy how to dress or act. Remember, he's your knight in shining armor! The cowboy who rescues the schoolmarm from the outlaws! You wanted a country man. Let him be country, and try a little on for size yourself.

On the other hand, maybe a few of his traits are legitimately hard to take. Is he so involved in work that you feel left out? Do you need more of his time? Maybe you'd like to be more involved in decision making—maybe less. Does he expect too much from you or not enough? Is he moving too fast or not fast enough? These kinds of issues should be addressed. The answers may require change by one of you, maybe both. But there's a big difference between asking a guy to change his personal habits and making changes to make your lives workable. The big things count. Let the little ones go.

Consider his habit of tracking mud in the kitchen—does it really bother you that much? After all, he came inside to spend time with you, didn't he? Just because he remembers the name of every animal on the place, but forgets your mother's, doesn't mean she isn't important. He's probably just forgetful, or it could be that your mother shares a name with someone from his past he'd rather forget. Don't make something like this into a big deal. On the other hand, it's important for each of you to both accept *and* get along with each other's families. In a case like this, a gentle reminder is certainly appropriate.

My country man is disorganized and has a habit of forgetting where he puts things. Instead of nagging or nitpicking, I consider his forgetfulness an endearing trait, sort of like a classic "absentminded professor." I don't expect him to change because I know he isn't going to. Why set both of us up to be unhappy? If your guy's a real-life version of Pigpen or a neatnick or he forgets to stop at the store, adopt a "that's how he is" attitude. After all, you may have little habits that annoy him, too. Does he nag you to tuck in your shirt or to remember to put the cap on the toothpaste tube? If he does, maybe he should read this chapter!

If, on the other hand, the things that bother you are big issues, you may want to rethink the relationship. If he drinks too much, is possessive or selfish, you have to decide whether you can (or should) put up with that. How about a demanding ex-wife and children who live a half mile away? You can't ask him to give up his children and, unfortunately, the ex-wife is part of the deal.

Decide whether you can accept his bad points along with the good before you've gone too far. You don't want to get hurt, and you don't want to invest too much in a relationship that hasn't got a future. There are plenty of other country men out there. You just have to find the right one.

CHAPTER 22

Love Wisely—Choose Passion over Romance

Love is one of those tricky words. How can someone "love" both ice cream and their mate? A good movie and their newborn baby? How can you compare "loving" working in the garden with "loving" your family? How can one word describe all those different feelings? I've heard that Eskimos have a dozen words in their language to describe "snow." I think there should be a dozen words to describe love. The same with passion. Mozart was passionate about music, van Gogh his art. Some people are passionate about causes (save the whale, spotted owl, or the environment), while some people think passion is limited to the bedroom.

Just so we both understand which variety of "love" and "passion" we're talking about, this is the heartfelt kind that engages your heart, mind, and senses. Love is caring deeply about someone. Wild, deep passion can last a lifetime. You can live without both, and either can change your life.

Romance is Valentine's Day, hearts and flowers, and a Technicolor sunset. Romance can be a flash of sizzling desire or butterfly flutters in the pit of your stomach. Romance is wonderful, but it's transitory. Although the feeling may remain in your memory, it passes through your life. That's not what you're looking for. You're looking for love for the long term, not a romantic tryst on Saturday night.

This isn't a game, and you aren't just flirting with the idea of finding love and a new life. You're serious, or you wouldn't be reading this book. Romance can carry you along on a thunderous roller-coaster ride. Sexual attraction can certainly be stimulating and, hopefully, very satisfying. But you can't base a marriage or life partnership on simply having a good time *or* good sex. That's what you *may* get when you have a hot date Friday night, and I'm all for that. But there comes a time when that's simply not enough. There comes a time when you want *more.*

Love *and* passion can be yours with a country man. Although he may seem like the strong, silent type, guess what? A country man experiences love and passion every day, and he's quite comfortable with the feeling. That gives him a head start on *expressing* those feelings. He's passionate about his ranch or business, his way of life, and the *country.* He loves his family, friends, and the animals he cares for every day. They all mean the world to him. Country Ways are part of your man, from the brim of his cowboy hat right down to his boots. Whether or not he's a cowboy isn't the point. He's *country*.

The country gives a man a natural outlet for his emotions. His love of the land and his feeling for the natural world give him a strong sense of purpose. He can be his own man, in his own way. You don't have to fit into a mold in the country, and that brings out the best in him. A country man can be comfortable in the role of nurturer and caregiver; he can also save lives. When you get down to the basics of life and death, you come face-to-face with yourself. Who you are. What you want. What you need. Love. Passion. Someone to come home to. Someone you care about.

Women yearn to have sweet nothings whispered in their ear. Sometimes we're disappointed. Sometimes men don't live up to our romantic expectations. Country men are better at *showing* than *telling*. Although they may bring you flowers, they wouldn't know the first thing about a love sonnet. Let's talk about how to recognize love, country style.

Love is being in town with your man and having him take your hand and hold on. Isn't it obvious he wants people to know how he feels? He isn't embarrassed that he wants to touch you. He wants everyone to know you belong with him. He's proud. He's *telling you* how much he loves you.

Love is being with a man who takes a child on a walk through a forest that's just been timbered. Listening to him explain why the startling scent of pine fills the air and why tree rings come in different sizes. Listening as he helps the child understand the significance of felling a hundred-year-old tree and how many years it will take to grow another. How could you not love this man?

No one is perfect at love or relationships. There isn't one surefire way or a tried-and-true method. All you can do is give it your best shot and love, support, and accept each other. Watch for the signs of love, the strike of passion. You don't want to miss them or overlook the little things. Be careful about love. Cherish the passion. As long as you're in this thing called love together, nothing can come between you.

CHAPTER 23

Finding Your Rhythm

John Wayne and Clint Eastwood are the classic stereotypes. Brad Pitt and Jimmy Smits offer a gentler version. Either way, most country men tap into our image of the "strong, silent type." Rugged, capable, and determined, they stand tall and have a rough-edged exterior. Clint and John are tough guys with a take-charge attitude. Brad and Jimmy are strong, too, but they have a gentler, tender side that can make a grown woman sigh.

You're probably attracted to one type or the other, just as you probably walk on the stronger or softer side of life. If you're a mild-mannered, easygoing woman, you may find it easier to adapt to the country. You'll most likely feel you've found the home sweet home you've always yearned for. But tenacious, strong-minded women may find their relationship with a country man more difficult. Why? Because strong people have a natural tendency to lead, and since there are two of you in the relationship, you may step on each other's toes.

You'll have to learn how to synchronize your steps while holding tight to each other—a sort of country version of Fred Astaire and Ginger Rogers. They had such symmetry and grace, they looked as if they'd been dancing together since birth. I wonder how many hours they practiced before taking those impressive and perfect whirls around the dance floor? That's about as long (and often) as two strong people have to practice until they get it right, too.

Getting things in sync include styles of communication. Strong men don't like to be told what to do, and I'm sure you don't, either. There are many ways to speak your mind without telling a man what to do. You can hint sweetly, talk around a given subject, ask directly, or even bat your baby blues. While each of those tactics may work in a given situation, I have another idea. Why not let him come to you for advice? How do you do that?

By playing the waiting game. By being supportive and not giving unsolicited advice.

Most men look for advice as a last resort and after they've done everything they can—alone. Sometimes it's hard to keep your own counsel, to wait things out and trust that someone besides yourself is going to solve a problem without your input. Sometimes you think it's your right or obligation to step in and take over. Try not to do that. Trust is a crucial part of any relationship.

Let him know you trust him by encouraging him to figure out the problem on his own.

Once a country man knows you're in his corner and that you have confidence in him, he's more likely to come to you for advice. I know that sounds somewhat contradictory, but it really isn't. When you give your man the opportunity to come to you, you've created the perfect opportunity to learn about him, appreciate him, *and* put in your two cents' worth—maybe three or four!

A gentler man is usually more communicative and open to discussion. He'll see the value to almost any point of view and listen eagerly to what you have to say. He may also express his feelings more often than the strong, silent type.

Whichever type of man you're with, if you're strong enough to stand back and let him come to you, you'll be on your way toward a good, solid relationship.

Women sometimes find it difficult to be quiet. I know I do. There's something about silence that makes me want to jump in and fill the void with noise. Small talk, chatter, anything. In the past few years I've realized that's a mistake.

Learning to take a deep breath and wait is a powerful tool. It gives your man time to mull things over and to feel comfortable asking for your advice. The good news is that *most* country men, whatever the type, are smart enough to know women are better at managing relationships than they are. Women have traditionally been the ones charged with keeping the family together, and most country men are happy to keep it that way. That doesn't mean he isn't interested or that he doesn't care. He just thinks you'll do a better job.

I do suggest you turn to him for advice. After all, country is his world, and you want to be part of it. You've got lots of questions. He's got lots of answers. If you didn't turn to him, it would be like going to a foreign country and *not* listening to your interpreter. Why would you do that? You're not going to understand the language. The culture is different. They even dress funny!

Why not make it easy on yourself and pay attention to the guy who's trying to explain things? If he has most of the information and knowledge, isn't it logical that he should be the one to take the lead? Shouldn't you be smart enough to let him?

My guy and I disagree, but we rarely argue. We talk about everything, and we have differing viewpoints, but we never go for the jugular. We never throw sarcastic words around because they can come back to haunt you. In any relationship, there are some words that cannot be taken back. There are some things that, once said, are never forgotten. You both need to be careful. Sometimes it's better to take a deep breath and swallow those hurtful thoughts.

 "If you can't say something nice, don't say anything at all"—an age-old cliché you need to acknowledge.

I know you want to be heard, but you don't want him to feel smothered. You want to help, but you don't need to shout. Don't try to solve his problems. After all, they are *his* problems. You have your own to deal with. Although he'll want to share good news with you, he'll also want to shield you from difficulties. It's his natural bent to want to both protect and impress you. After all, you're his woman! Would I be going too far to suggest you should encourage and nourish his pursuit of *your* happiness? No, I didn't think so!

My country man and I could both be described in similar terms—intelligent, capable, and quite comfortable making decisions. You could even say we're bullheaded. The first couple of years we were together were difficult. But, as in any successful relationship, love, hard work, and commitment kept us together until we found our rhythm. Don't be discouraged if it takes you a while—whether it's a Texas two-step or a slow country serenade, you will find a rhythm all your own. And I guarantee it will be worth the wait.

Chapter 24

Catch a Country Star

Love is in the air, and you're blissfully happy. You've found the country guy of your dreams, you're keeping company and spending weekends together. It's time to take a deep breath and ask yourself some hard questions. More important, it's time for some answers. Whether you're still living in the city or have already moved to the country, you need to decide if you're ready to make a commitment to this man. If you're still in the city, the question is even harder because it brings up a dozen more. Is the time right? Are you ready? Will you be quitting your job, starting a new one, or keeping the home fires burning? Are you ready for life to change *big* time?

In either case, if you've decided you have a real shot at happiness with this man and his way of life, what comes next? What you've been waiting for all this time—the courtship dance!

By this point in the relationship, both of you need and count on each other. He looks to you for emotional comfort, and his strength is integral to your happiness. Your life is exceptionally busy, especially if you're commuting to the country on weekends. He's busy, too, and he misses you terribly. That's too bad. It's also *essential.* He needs to see a big, black hole in his life that only *you* can fill.

How do you get him to take the next, giant step?

Country men are shy, and when it comes to women, some are downright tongue-tied. They may stumble over their words when it comes to popping the question. They may not even ask unless they see clear signals that the answer will be "yes." Getting them to say the words is partly your job. How do you do that?

Don't bring up living together, how he feels about commitments, or whether he prefers June or December weddings.

Although this might seem contradictory, it isn't. Most men like to do the chasing, and one thing they don't like is ultimatums. You just need to take the relationship a step *backward* and slow down the pace a bit. If your country beau needs a gentle nudge, just remind him that absence *does* make the heart grow fonder. You can do that by filling your days with interesting activities and making occasional plans to do something by yourself or with a friend. Be sure to let your man know what you're doing in a matter-of-fact way. Don't make it sound as if you're making plans without him because you're unhappy. You aren't. You're doing something *separately* simply because you *are* still separate.

He may feel somewhat confused by this turn of events, and he probably won't like it. But he'll also come to the realization that he can solve his dilemma of not having you by his side—all he has to do is make a commitment. By letting him figure this out (instead of telling him), he'll always remember it was *his* idea to do the catching, not the other way around.

Another tip: If you haven't already moved to the country, why not start your plans with or without him?

He may not be certain you're really serious about trading in your city existence for country life, so why not make the move and prove it to him? I recommend this only if you're sure country life is for you, man or no man. You'll probably find that if you're going to be living in town and *available,* he'll have a strong incentive to pop the question. After all, you're a terrific woman. Sweet and shy, independent and outgoing, or anywhere in between, there aren't many women like you around his neck of the woods.

Another way to show him you want to be caught is to do little things that tell him you appreciate him.

Call him "honey," take an interest in everything he does, and fix man-size lunches on days he's headed out to mend a half mile of fenceline. Let him know you care, whether your style is a shy kiss, gazing up at him through dewy lashes, or hot, steamy sex. Remember, he's your hero!

How about getting up early to help feed the animals or asking him to show you how to curry the horses? One of my favorite things to do is tag along on the back of the tractor when my guy's out in the fields. That may sound crazy to you, but I enjoy time with my man, whenever and however we find it. These suggestions are all unmistakable declarations of love and commitment to him and his way of life. You're telling him it's okay to pop the question because you're going to say "yes"!

Start leaving a few things at his place.

Keeping company is reason enough to leave your toothbrush and a few other personal items in his bedroom or bath. What's the point of dragging your muck boots (calf-high rubbers worn when mucking through animal pens) back to the city? Don't leave so much stuff that it seems as if you've moved in. Women have a tendency to "nest" and "make a house a home." Don't do that . . . not yet! I know you love him, but how comfortable do you want him to be with this *pre*nuptial state? If you leave only a few essential things, you'll give him a small taste of what it's like to have you around. At the same time, he'll have a subtle reminder that you have a separate life that doesn't include him.

Giving him *less* than what he wants will help motivate him to make the relationship permanent.

In this case, he can't have you in his house, his bed, and his life because of the distance factor. Even if you've moved to the country *before* you met him, you're not the type of woman to live your life for weekends. You want and deserve more than that. Seeing him only on weekends is the perfect way to make his heart grow fonder—and yours, too. When you have five harried days to muddle through before seeing your beloved, won't the waiting be harder? When you have only two nights together, won't the loving be longer?

It's important to have an "understanding" before deciding to live together.

Whether that's an engagement, commitment, or marriage is up to you. You're both grown-ups, and you can make that decision on your own. So when I say, "Help him pop the question," I'm not restricting the question to "Will you marry me?" It could just as well be "Spend your life with me" or both. I do believe this is *your* call. He should do whatever makes *you* happy. My guess is he'll prefer to slip a wedding band on your finger to just living together. Country Ways are traditional, and he's probably a traditional guy.

If you prefer some other arrangement, he'll probably go along because he loves *you* more than he loves traditions. But be warned—you may have to explain yourself to his family; they're sure to want to usher you into the family with an old-fashioned country wedding!

Section Three

Adjusting to Country Life

CHAPTER 25

Keep the Home Fires Burning

Now that you've got your country man, it's important to keep him happy. What's that? you say. Haven't I done enough already? I've completely changed my life for this guy! Shouldn't he be worrying about how to keep me happy? Absolutely! But you've been so busy, you may not have noticed how hard he's working to make room for you in his life.

One area that may be difficult for him is integrating you smoothly into his country lifestyle. Outside pressure can make this tough. Can't you just hear the neighbors wondering how he's going to keep that city gal happy now that she's down on the farm? How you react to being the new kid in town is important. Your behavior around others is the key to whether or not they accept you—and believe me, their acceptance can mean the difference between success and failure in your new country life.

Don't act as if the country is just another stop on your busy agenda—let people know you love your new life, are positive about whatever your new country life throws your way and that your man means more to you than *any*thing you left behind in the city.

Do *not* pepper your conversations with, "That's not how we do it in the city," or, "I can show you an easier way [a better way or newer method]."

Let country people know you're eager to have them show you *their* way—they'll be flattered by your respect and look more kindly on your arrival. Your man can't protect you from yourself, and he can't shield and protect you from this "outsider" tag if you sandbag him. I know you don't understand the effect some city attitudes can have on country folk, but remember, you *are* quite a handful! Isn't that one reason your country beau fell head over heels in love with you?

And that brings me to something else you should keep in mind as your relationship develops—remember why he was attracted to you in the first place. If it was your independent attitude and fighting spirit, direct those energies toward your new country life. If it was your gentleness and quiet nature, let those qualities shine. Whether it's starting your own business, volunteering in the community or at school, being a partner in his ranch, or bringing peace to his surroundings, give it all you've got. Shine like a star if you dream big dreams, glitter like stardust if that's more your style.

No matter what your personality, or what role you play in your new country life, it's a good idea to maintain a few separate interests.

I enjoy spending time with my man, but everybody needs to get away from home once in a while. Whether it's lunching with a friend, checking out a new business in town, or simply going for a walk to gather wildflowers, save some time for yourself.

I'm one of those energetic, type-A personalities. If I don't get away occasionally, I go stir-crazy. If I can't come up with a *legitimate* reason, I find any old excuse and announce, "I'm getting the hell out of Dodge!" My man knows me well enough to smile sweetly and wave as I head down the driveway. He knows I'll return with a *much* better attitude. That's one reason I love him—he puts up with me!

The good news is that although country men work hard, they also like to play. It's just that they sometimes have to be reminded, and that's where you can make a difference.

Come up with something that's fun, sweet, or thoughtful to do *for* him and *with* him.

Plan it around a work activity, and you've got it made. He'll be surprised and delighted that you thought of him. He'll enjoy having you show up where he's working, because it shows you appreciate his work (ten extra points for you!).

- How about preparing a special picnic basket for two?

Throw a saddle on your favorite horse (or jump in the pickup) and ride out in the fields, to the north forty, on the range, or a short hop, skip, and jump to the barn or corrals—wherever he's working. Crook your finger in his direction, smile sweetly (or suggestively), and he's yours! If he works in town, drop into his office right before lunch and meander over to the local park or the courthouse square. Spread a blanket on the lawn, cradle his head in your lap, and feed him bonbons. Everyone will see what a terrific woman you are and how much you adore him. Another ten points!

- Go hunting, fishing, or riding with him Saturday morning. Wanting to be with him shows how much you love him.
- Cook dinner, make his house your *home,* get along with his mother, enjoy his dad's corny jokes, and don't side with your kids against him.
- Wear sexy underwear and soft, cotton nightshirts in pretty colors.
- Kiss him first thing in the morning and the last thing at night.

Country men hold a picture close to their hearts—it's you the first day you met. That's the way he'll always remember you—the way the sun glinted on your hair, the sweet curve of your smile, the sound of your voice. You were the woman he wanted more than any other. You were the woman he fought for and won. Isn't that romantic? When he's on his way home, that picture will be imprinted in his mind.

You look forward to seeing your guy—doesn't he deserve to know that? To see those feelings expressed in your smile, your glance, and a welcoming kiss? Remember, he has that image of *wonderful* you imprinted in his brain. That's the way you *want* him to remember you. Too many women complain that the romance dwindles after the first few months of a relationship. I think women have the know-how to keep that romance alive. All it takes is a little attention to detail.

Do *not* roll your eyes when he comes in after working a ten-hour day, muddy and dirty, smelling like cattle, horses, alfalfa, peaches, apples, or onions.

He *will* see the expression on your face. You should be proud of how hard he works. That's what makes the ranch or farm run. He *will* be sweaty. He *will* be gritty. Never make him feel he's too grungy to sit on the furniture. Buy or make slipcovers. Better yet, designate one chair as "his."

Remember, his home is his castle. He chose you to be his queen, not his keeper. Besides, if you're working with him, you'll smell as bad as he does. Remember, this is an equal partnership, and it may be a toss of the coin to see who gets the shower first. Better yet, save water—shower together!

I think women underestimate the power they can wield in a relationship. Show your guy that you appreciate and admire him and he'll work like hell for you and your family. Work *alongside* him and you'll earn his love and respect. If your talents or abilities lie elsewhere, that's okay, too. How you blend the relationship is up to you. Together, working as a team, you and your man can make Country Ways the best thing that ever happened to *both* of you.

CHAPTER 26

Small-Town Gossip and Taking Sides

We've already mentioned that you will be under close scrutiny as the "new kid in town." Coming from a big anonymous city, this may surprise you, but consider yourself warned—in small towns everybody knows everybody. You can't keep to yourself, and you wouldn't want to. Living in a close-knit community means your business and personal life aren't necessarily private. Most people are naturally curious, and country folk are no different. People will want to know who you are, what you're doing, and how you're going to affect their lives and their town.

If you think that seems ludicrous, think again. You may not *intend* to change anyone's life except your own (and that of your country guy), but that's not how it's going to be. One person really *can* make a difference in a small town. Most of the time that's good, but sometimes it isn't, and from anyone's perspective, *inquiring minds want to know!*

People will be curious about you from the start, but once you make the big move, they'll be quite serious about getting to know you. They'll invite you places and suggest you get involved in community affairs. Whether you move to town, into your new man's life, or both, you will be grist for the rumor mill. *Who is she? Why did she move here? Where is she from? What's she like? Will we like her? Will she like us?*

The good news is that people will know when your business is booming, your favorite filly took blue ribbons at the county fair, little Susie has been named Student of the Month, and you've sold your latest book. The bad news is that you can't run and you can't hide. In small towns everyone also knows if business is bad, wheat prices have plummeted (and that's your main source of income), and your teenage son got a speeding ticket. Try to take it in stride. At some point you *will* be embarrassed, you *will* get over it, and life *will* go on. Gossiping is often a response to insecurity or a reaction to change. Change is scary, whether you're insecure or not. Instead of getting annoyed at an inevitable fact of life, let's take a look at how to make the situation work for, instead of against, you.

I've found the most effective method of dealing with small-town gossip is to be as open and honest as possible.

Take control of the rumor mill by telling people what they want to know, in your own way and on your own terms. You have nothing to gain by letting them guess, but you do have something to lose—your chance to tell it as it is. I suggest you go with the sports axiom "The best defense is a good offense" and head those rumors off at the pass. You will be asked personal questions, and you will be asked about your beau and your relationship. How you answer depends on how you view these private matters. I draw the line at explaining my feelings (or my guy's) to *anybody*, and most important, I consider how he'd feel about my confiding anything of a personal nature.

However, I *would* talk about a lot of other things: how you met, what you have in common, your career move, hobbies—you know the kinds of things I'm talking about. Otherwise I suggest "dodging the bullet." I'm not backing off my advice to be as open and honest as possible, but I don't think you should invite anyone into the *privacy* of your relationship. Keep in mind that trust is of paramount importance between you and your man, and once lost, is extremely difficult to regain.

Politics and family feuds like those between the Hatfields and the McCoys are alive and well in the country. As in lots of small towns, there will be families who've been around for generations and are important to the community in one way or another. Then there are those new to town and those who've been around a few years. More often than not, the "sides" of an issue don't make a lot of sense to newcomers because they don't understand the history of the issue or the families involved. This is *not* something you can learn easily or quickly. Talk to your country man and your friends, then straddle the fence. Yes, you heard right. My advice is to *not* take a stand. At least not yet.

In addition to all the typical subjects of gossip—love affairs, family squabbles, success, failure, and politics—there is another area of discussion that's a pretty hot topic in the country: land use issues. Here are some strategies to help you navigate what is probably a foreign topic but one you shouldn't underestimate.

While a hundred acres may sound like heaven to you, in some parts of the country it's hardly worth talking about. When you're living in a city apartment, five acres sounds like a lot. When you live in an area that bases its economy on agriculture, cattle, or sheep, acreage may be counted in the hundreds or thousands. Twenty acres is about the smallest parcel that can sustain a farm or ranch, although you can certainly live comfortably with five. When adjoining acreage goes up for sale, you will immediately understand the concept of land envy and where your savings are headed!

A word of advice: "Subdivide" is a dirty word to country folk.

It conjures up visions of housing tracts filled with ticky-tacky houses that all look alike. When a neighbor files a petition to subdivide his land into fewer than twenty acres, you can expect a feud. On the one hand, your neighbor has a right to make money off his land, and there's probably a realtor or developer offering him a stack of greenbacks. On the other, you don't want ten or twenty neighbors when now you have one. The debate *will* be heated!

Again, until you understand all the issues, my advice is to *not* take sides. Listen, ask questions, and gather information. If it's a public hearing, I would advise against speaking for or against anybody. If it's a vote, by all means mark your ballot, but you might not want to tell people which box you checked. You're going to live here a long time, and you don't want to alienate anybody. One day you might want those people on *your* side of an issue.

CHAPTER 27

Don't Look Back

You've swallowed hard and taken that leap of faith. Whether you made the move on your own or found that special guy first, you're starting a new life in the country. That life is probably radically different from the one you lived in the city, and that calls for some radical thought. Let's take stock of where we are on the road that leads to the "country side of love," then talk about a few basics that should help keep you on course.

The first is changing your point of view about your comfort zone.

In this case, what's easiest is *not* what's best. Remember Linus from the comic strip *Peanuts*? He carried his security blanket everywhere because it made him feel safe and warm. Taking that first (second and third) step into the unknown means leaving your security behind and embracing this brave, new world.

The road may be smooth, it may be filled with twists and turns, or you may be in for a few hard landings. The point is, you no longer have all the answers. The good news is, you only have to look in new directions to find what you need. Those new avenues include your country man, neighbors, friends, and community.

The second basic premise is to leave the past behind.

Yes, you have friends back in the city who are important to you. Yes, they've accepted that you're serious about this "country thing," but it's probably also true that they're dubious at best. When you talk about getting up at dawn with your guy and glorying in the beauty of a sunrise, will they think you've gone over the edge? When you plant a spring garden, bake a pie, learn to ride, or help calves come into the world, will they share your joy or laugh out loud?

How will your best chum react when you tell her about "bumper sheep," which happens when winter ices everything up, including the road leading from the sheep pens to the feeding area? The sheep get so excited when the dinner bell rings, and are in such a hurry, they pick up speed, slip on the ice, and crash into each other—much like a carnival bumper pool ride. (No, the sheep don't get hurt.) Will she roll her eyes in disbelief? Will she start calling you her "country cousin"?

Don't think you'll be left completely alone. I'm certain a few of your friends will share your enthusiasm for Country Ways. My good friend Sheila thought the move (and my man) were wonderful, and she encouraged me to try anything and everything that passed my way. When we talk on the phone, she loves to hear the sheep baaing or Savannah barking in the background. Last year I sent Sheila a few skeins of yarn I'd spun from the fleece of one of my favorite ewes, Kiss Kiss. After knitting the wool into a vest, Sheila asked for a photo of Kiss Kiss, which she proudly displays on her refrigerator door.

Prepare yourself for disparaging remarks about lack of culture, "hillbilly heaven," and what it must really be like "down on the farm."

You may feel as if they're humoring you, and you may not like that. You'll want to share this new life and the "new you" with them, while they'll want to fill you in on office politics and gossip. You'll be eager to share the benefits of small-town life, while they'll want to remind you of everything you're missing.

This may be a difficult time for both you and your city friends. The chances of them understanding your newfound point of view are slim. As long as they're caught up in the noise, frenetic pace, and deadlines that are so much a part of the city, I don't know if they *can* get it. I'm not saying your friends don't have the best of intentions, or that they don't care, but keep in mind that in some ways you've deserted them. Don't be disappointed if you don't get the reaction you're looking for, and be forewarned that their advice may not be of much help. After all, they don't know much (if anything) about Country Ways. But don't be too hard on them. Remember, you used to be city yourself. Console yourself with the knowledge that you're forging ahead into new territory!

Last, keep your eyes focused on the future.

In some part, you must break with the past before you can forge ahead. I'm not saying to give up your city friends completely, but you may find that those who encouraged your weekend forays to the country are suddenly unsupportive. In some ways you can't blame them. You see, by choosing to leave the city, you're saying there *is* a better way to live. That also says something negative about what you've left behind. Since your friends have chosen to remain, your leaving is a way of saying you've found fault with *their* choice.

So how do you handle the struggles and the push and pull of your heartstrings while making all these changes? A delicate balance is needed here, and it may take a while to find your footing. In time I'm sure you'll be able to pull it off, but for now, why not try juggling? Just keep one eye on all you have to look forward to and the other firmly in the here-and-now.

- Look in your own backyard for guidance—first to your new partner, then to the new friends you're making.

Chances are, your "country connections" understand what you're going through and do want to help. More important, they're in the best position to offer good, sound advice. Form friendships in the country, and the sooner the better. I know it's not easy, and it won't be the same for a while, but it *is* in your best interests over the long term.

- Reach out to people, invite them to your home, and accept invitations to theirs.

Become part of the community, and in no time at all you'll have country friends for the choosing. Keep in mind that there are some important differences between city and country friendships. In the city, there may be external reasons for forming friendships—you either work together or go to the same gym, hairdresser, art class, and so on. Don't get me wrong—having something in common is a good reason for getting to know someone. But country friendships are different because these are the people you'll be sharing your *life* with, not just small parts of it. Country friendships are different for another, very important reason—they're predicated on sharing some very basic and important beliefs in a way of life.

That's a constant, no matter who you are, what you do for a living, what size house you live in, or whether you have children. The more you understand, accept, and appreciate this concept, the quicker you'll be accepted by other country folk and feel right at home.

CHAPTER 28

Never Judge a Book By Its Cover

At this point, it should come as no surprise when I say that country folk aren't as quick to judge on appearances as city dwellers seem to be. That may seem like a trivial point, but it isn't. How you perceive people—and their reaction to that perception—are key elements to your success in any country community. You start earning your country reputation the minute you come to town, and how you put that first foot forward is important. Country folk have long memories, and although relationships have an impact on how things are accomplished in both city and country, there are significant differences in approach.

In the country you should treat everyone as if they're a treasured friend you've known for years.

Business and personal relationships are intertwined by definition—if you have no friends, you have no business connections. In the city there's a new customer walking in the door every day. In the country your customer is your neighbor. You need him, and he needs you. Understanding and accepting that difference will make or break your transition from city to country.

When you go to the bank, hardware store, or grocery store, treat the employees like friends. Ask, "How are you?" and really mean it.

Country folk can easily recognize a newcomer who's all business, because Country Ways are more easygoing and friendly than city attitudes. Take your time, slow down. It'll all work out. And remember, you never know whom you're talking to. In my town, doctors and lawyers may wear well-worn jeans both in the office *and* after hours, and the man stocking shelves in the hardware store may own not only the store, but half the buildings in town! It's a mistake to judge a country man by the clothes he wears.

The first time sheep shearers came to the ranch, I didn't pay much attention. They were a husband-wife team in their forties, looking about how you'd expect sheep shearers to look—grungy. I later found out *she* was one of our county commissioners! This year the shearer was a rugged, handsome guy around thirty, dressed in faded jeans and shirt and driving a five-year-old pickup. He also owns a thousand-acre ranch and runs a "band" of sheep (anything over five hundred) and about eight hundred goats. Shearing his own sheep is a matter of pride, but he also has a team of shearers that covers three states. When he shears, he evaluates each sheep as he goes along and gives advice on herd management. He's a successful businessman by any standards. He's also single.

Country people wear more than one hat—sometimes three or four.

Your next-door neighbor may be your barber, but he may also be the sheriff or a doctor. Small-town folk may become your friends, or they may drive you to distraction. Either way, you'll run into them at the grocery store and the beauty shop, the library and the post office. Your doctor may coach Little League, and the mayor will be a member of the local Parent Teacher Association.

The owner of a small convenience store in a nearby village is also a member of our county Land Use Commission. Although her days are spent stocking shelves and running a cash register, once a week she casts her vote on important issues, including countywide zoning changes. The foreman on a local power company crew may install new electrical service to customers, but he was also recently elected to a term as one of three county commissioners. When his crew comes up to repair our lines, we make sure to go out for a neighborly chat. Then we brew a pot of coffee, fill a big thermos, and take it out to the crew.

You never know when your good (or bad) manners will be remembered, and you never know just whom it is you may be talking to.

Our county sheriff is one of the few women police chiefs in the United States. She's thirtysomething, third-generation country, and you're welcome in her office any time. She has a smile for everyone and is sure to remember your name. She won out over the incumbent—a good old country boy. He'd been a good deputy, but some people thought winning the office of sheriff gave him an inflated sense of self-importance. That didn't sit well with his neighbors. When the voters had an opportunity to remind him that "those who giveth can also taketh away," they did.

Even though you're going through some big changes in this move from city to country, remember who you are and what you stand for. People will form impressions about you from the first day they tip their hat, shake your hand, or do business with you in the grocery store. You want that first impression to be a good one, so it's important to keep your eyes set on your goals while keeping your feet firmly on the ground. Treat everyone with equal kindness and candor, and you shouldn't have any problems.

CHAPTER 29

Country Men Aren't Big Spenders, but They Have Hearts of Gold

Talking about money is one of those *touchy* subjects—so let's get right down to it. Everybody has a personal idea about what to spend money on, what's important and what isn't. I think everybody would agree that money is one of the biggest areas of conflict between men and women. The country isn't any different. What *is* different is Country Ways. If you're going to make the change from city to country and keep the harmony of your relationship intact, you need to be aware of the dollars and *sense* of rural life.

Have you ever driven down a country road and seen a small herd of cattle grazing in the distance? You probably didn't give much thought to what that represents to the rancher. I suggest you take another look—those are thousand-dollar bills wandering around the countryside. Cattle are *big* business. The same can be said for all kinds of livestock, agriculture, and other rural-based operations or businesses. There's money to be made in the country, but as the old saying goes, "It takes money to make money." There are veterinarian bills, feed costs, and upkeep for repairs and purchasing of machinery and equipment.

Weather has a direct effect on agricultural profits, too. If it's a good year and there's a bumper wheat crop, grain prices go down. That's good for the livestock owner but bad for the wheat farmer. If you or your man owns a small business, the local economy will affect your profit-and-loss statement. If he's an attorney, accountant, or doctor, your neighbor's cash flow will have a direct impact on your country man's business. Life isn't compartmentalized in the country; it's interconnected.

The cycles of life and the environment are important factors in country living. You have to manage both the good and bad times. Your life and your success will, to some degree, be intertwined with the community. That makes people cautious. Country folk tend to be savers, whether it's money, a year's worth of canned food, fabric remnants for quilting, or replacement parts for machinery. Country folk have been through lean times before and know those times will come again. What does this mean for you? You need to learn to adjust your spending within cycles and be prepared for the future.

Planning ahead is your best defense.

Consider using "home-grown" talents and skills to bring in extra income. My friend Cindy plants a huge garden every spring—everything from vegetables to edible flowers. Not only does she enjoy gardening, she knows her family will have a wonderful supply of fresh produce throughout the year. When Cindy had too much food for her family's table, she used to give it away, but now she's started her own business selling her prize-winning jams and jellies, dilly beans, zucchini, and asparagus. "Cindy Lynn's Country Kitchen" has been so successful, she's considering expanding her product line to include herbs fresh from the garden. And that's more money to put aside for both necessities and the little luxuries that are so important to us all.

When times are good, country folk take a satisfied breath and catch up on their spending.

Be aware that a country man has certain priorities for ready cash—land, land, and more land! Next comes livestock, feed, equipment, and tools. But this isn't necessarily bad. If your country man enjoys working with wood, you may get custom-made furniture from oak trees growing right on your property instead of a table or bureau bought in a store. What greater treasure than a hand-hewn desk or dresser to hand down to your children and their children?

A country man will buy a portion of his equipment and machinery at auction, but every rancher has to have a John Deere (that's tractor in city talk). I'd compare my man's excitement to buying a backhoe with most women's thrill at getting a five-carat diamond ring. If you want country, go for the backhoe. If you've got your heart set on five carats, you might be better off in the city. When it comes to a best friend, I'd choose my man over a diamond any day.

Country men are serious about their responsibility toward family, and that means you. However, a country man's ability to increase his income does mean reinvestment, in both time and money. Country does *not* mean low income. It *does* mean taking a look at your priorities and how and why you spend and save money. If you carefully examine your spending needs, you may find you can make do with five sweaters instead of fifteen. I might add that when shopping is forty minutes away instead of ten, you're more likely to resist impulse buying. When you're not commuting to and from work, you also don't pass by shopping malls. That helps put temptation out of reach!

We may not like to think about it, but there is an emotional component to shopping. Purchasing power can be like a quick fix or temporary thrill. Shopping feels good while you're doing it, but you may end up with buyer's remorse once you get home or the credit card bills come in.

Spending money isn't a means to happiness.

Spending *time* with someone, creating something beautiful with your hands, giving of yourself—those are the kinds of things that bring real happiness. Recalling the warmth and simplicity of an earlier time may help you understand what I'm talking about. My grandparents lived in a small town in Missouri, and my sister and I visited for a month every summer when we were growing up. The things I remember most, and that had lasting impact on my life, had nothing to do with money. I remember morning walks to the bakery for strudel still warm from the oven, going fishing with my grandfather, and bringing our catch of the day home for dinner. I especially remember Grandmother teaching me to sew on her treadle sewing machine. I must have been only eight or nine years old, but those lessons sparked an interest in fiber, color, and design that continues today.

We all know money can't buy happiness, create lasting memories, or teach life's important lessons. For that you need time, love, and the desire and will to make it happen. You can't find those things in a wallet, but you *can* find them with Country Ways. This is your opportunity to find what's been missing in your life, to reach inside yourself to build your own memories, and to create them with your children.

If you shop out of habit rather than need, you might want to consider cultivating a new habit: hone your creative skills instead of trooping through the malls.

Things that are made by hand not only have the *cachet* of being more valuable, they are! If you want a new centerpiece for your dining room table, explore your own backyard. Gather pinecones and boughs of blue spruce, pick wildflowers, and use a cream pitcher as a vase. Do anything, but use your imagination rather than your wallet. Bake loaves of cranberry or banana walnut cake for hostess gifts, turn cotton nightgowns into heirlooms by sewing yards of inexpensive lace on the hems. Turn everyday things into marvels of creativity that are a direct expression of you.

Once you make the change, you'll discover an extra bonus—holidays are a completely different experience! No guilt, no returning presents you don't want or need, never a feeling of "Is that all there is?" Instead you have time to decorate your home, make birthday cards, bake special meals and desserts, and be creative in whatever way suits your fancy.

Another cutback strategy is to dump all the mail-order catalogs in the trash and ignore advertising campaigns aimed at emptying your wallet.

Don't tell yourself you can't afford it—remind yourself you don't need it. Maybe you don't even want it! If you're shopping just out of habit, think of all the other things you can do with that shopping time and cold, hard cash.

Find happiness in simple things.

Enjoy a sunset tinged with shades of pink and gold, making new friends, sipping hot cocoa by a blazing fire, watching your children grow up safe and happy, sleeping in your lover's arms. Pamper yourself with a long, relaxing bath, fill a tiny silk bag with flowers from the garden and tuck it in your lingerie drawer, or relax with tea made from herbs from your own garden. Discover all the ways you can feel rich that don't cost money. Discover the joys of simplicity!

Your man *will* be careful with money. Taking care of things, whether it's problems or people, is a matter of pride for country men. In order to do that, he needs resources. He won't be a big spender, but he will be a careful one. He isn't *cheap,* but he does believe in saving for a rainy day. One of his strongest needs is to build a secure home for his family, one that will last a lifetime. That's where he'll gladly invest his time and money. That heart of gold stems from his desire to protect and care for his woman, his family, and his home. It's important that you understand your country man's fundamental, down-to-earth attitude toward money. Better yet, embrace it and make it part of your nature, too.

CHAPTER 30

Country Men Will Take an Interest in Your Children

If you have kids, you may be wondering how a move to the country will affect their lives. While the adjustments may be difficult, there's no question about it, raising children in the country is a good thing. Country living is about kids, Sunday dinners, community, faith, family, and friends. Kids go with small towns like Mom and apple pie, whether they're cute four-year-olds or rebellious teens. If the city leaves you dancing as fast as you can, your family may be more about microwave meals and cable TV than a quality life. So if a change of lifestyle is one of the main reasons you want to move to the country, you're on the right track. The nature of city life makes it difficult for families to spend a lot of time together, but Country Ways are quite different.

I think one reason for that difference has to do with distance—your next-door neighbors may live a half mile or more away! That may sound like country folk don't have much choice in this "together" concept, and that's partially true. More important, the logical outcome is that families spend a lot of time together.

You learn to talk to each other, depend on each other, and act as a team. That results in a better understanding of each other, including your strengths and weaknesses. This understanding goes a long way toward creating stronger bonds, both as a couple and as a family. The long days of summer, and even longer winter nights, result in great opportunities to spend time with your kids. When was the last time your family got together for the evening, made popcorn (the old-fashioned way instead of microwaved), and passed the bowl around—unless it was in a movie theater? And even then, did your kids sit next to you or down front?

If your children spend more time in their room (or on the Internet) than with you, the country will entice them outside. After all, there will be dogs to play with, horses to ride, chickens to feed, and so much to do! Your little computer genius may be interested in setting up a program to track crop or pasture rotations, cattle breeding, or his own business plan. Just because you're "down on the farm" doesn't mean you're not part of the computer age. On the contrary, I use the Internet for research, to market handcrafted products and fiber arts, and for keeping an eye on publishing trends. Our schools and small branch libraries have computers and Internet access, too.

Another reason your family will be closer is that you'll be more aware of what your kids are up to, where they are, and who they're with, because they'll have *fewer* choices on how to spend their time. This is definitely a case where less is *better* than more. Country living, by its very nature, gives you more to do at home. Whether it's caring for the land (five acres or five thousand), animals, crops, gardening, craftwork, parenting, or running a business, home will be the center of operations. That mechanism is built right in; you only have to use it to your best advantage.

When should you introduce your kids to your country love? When your country beau invites you to his ranch, farm, or country house. That's his way of saying he wants to make you part of his life. Showing you his place is, for a man, the same as you introducing him to your children. He hopes you find the land beautiful and the structures sound. You hope he's impressed that your twelve-year-old is smart, not that he sometimes has a smart mouth; or that he's charmed by your four-year-old's curiosity, not irritated that she gets into everything.

If you're a single mom with children, they're part of the package. I don't think you should introduce your kids to every man you meet, but about the time you're thinking about keeping company, it's an important step. You're deciding whether two lives can mesh into one, and that may include children—yours *or* his. Besides, he's sure to want to be part of *anything* you care about. Remember, he's *country,* and family is important.

Don't be shy in accepting an invitation to bring your children to the ranch.

Kids don't seem to be underfoot in the country the way they sometimes are in the city. There's plenty of room to roam, and besides, they'll be outside checking the place out. What if your kids dislike him right off? What if little Shannon thinks his clothes are funny, and ten-year-old Paul doesn't *want* a new father? Or maybe they want a dad so much that they cling to him like cocker spaniels? What if they make pests of themselves or, worse, are rude and hostile? What if his kids make fun of your citified ways and Nintendo-literate children?

I suggest you shrug your shoulders and give up the thought of peace on earth *and* the domestic front. Expect the worst, and things are bound to get better! If you didn't think this was worth fighting for, you wouldn't have started down the country road. Just keep going. You're on the right track. I can't think of a single mom who doesn't think her kids would be better off having a *good* father, and country men are good fathers. It doesn't matter if the kids are yours or his. They're *family,* and that means he'll feel responsible for them. You may have different styles, but you'll parent together.

Until you've gotten a handle on the parenting issue, you should both make a point of backing each other up in front of the kids. If you have a problem with something he's said to your children, discuss it with him in private.

Your kids may resent his stepping in at first, and he may do things completely differently from you, but it's important to encourage him. Give yourself time to work things out. Your kids (and his) will come around.

Larry, one of our local business owners, married Jo Anne, a single mom with two sons, a few years ago. Fifteen-year-old Josh didn't like the idea of a stepfather. As the eldest, he'd felt like "the man of the house" since his mom's divorce three years earlier. Jo Anne did count on Josh, and it was easy to understand why he felt threatened. The situation got worse when Larry nixed Josh's request for a car so he wouldn't have to ride the bus to school. Big-city kids may be used to public transportation, but suburban teenagers are used to having access to "wheels." In the country they don't. Things finally settled down when Larry offered Josh a job (at minimum wage) so he could save to buy a car in a year or so. Things still aren't perfect, but Josh's attitude has improved, and Larry's doing his best to work things out.

Sam, twelve, took to country life like a duck to water. About a month after the wedding, Larry asked Sam to go fishing. It was just the two of them—no big brother, no mom, and no wife. Jo Anne worried most of the day. What if Sam acted up? What if Larry lost his patience? What if they had an argument? What happened was that they came back best buddies. Larry and Sam spent the day together, and a little one-on-one seemed to do the trick.

Country men understand that children need a father. If your children have a good relationship with their biological father, you'll *all* have to get in on the juggling act. Joint parenting *can* be a good thing! If your children's natural father is the absent type, your country partner will step right in. But be prepared, because he'll take his new role seriously.

If you're used to making all the decisions, it's important to bring your man into the picture.

If he's new to parenting, you'll have to teach him the ropes. Remember, you're all in this together. We don't get to choose our families—we're stuck with them. But we do get to choose what we make of them. They can shelter us from life's storms and give us the freedom to follow our dreams. They can give us comfort and hope when everything else may be in chaos. Families can build a foundation for the future, and if it's love that makes the world go around, families are what hold it together.

That comes full circle in the context of a small community, because *we're* the ones who make our corner of the world work the way we want it to. Some people think country living is isolated, but I think of it as *insulated*—a protected, comfortable place where life is valued for what we make of it, not what *it* makes of *us*. A place where nurturing is a given, there's room to learn and grow, spread your wings and fly! I know that's what you want and the kind of life you want for your children. All you need is the chance, the time, and the country.

CHAPTER 31

Helping Your Children Adjust

Remember, if you have children, it's not just you who'll have to adjust; your children are in for some changes, too. You already know Country Ways are culturally different from city life, and one of those differences is the "village" concept. You've heard the saying "It takes a whole village to raise a child." Small towns have been raising kids that way for centuries.

Ranch hands, teachers, the school bus driver, and lots of other people will feel quite comfortable letting your child know if he's out of line.

It's like having a small army of adults watching out for everybody's kids. Don't be surprised if your children don't like this village concept. All those eyes on them? Someone knowing what they're doing all the time? Not being able to get away with anything? Yep! These changes will be tough on them, but then, being a single parent is tough on *you*. When you can spread the responsibility (and the love) around, the job becomes a lot easier and a lot more fun.

You'll be on a first-name basis with teachers, school counselors, and the principal, and you'll know your children's friends *and* their parents.

That's just part of living in a small community. Your children will eventually get used to the idea that everybody will know if they misbehave. That usually happens when they realize that when they do something good, everybody knows that, too. We all like to be told when we're doing a good job, and kids are no exception. Our local newspaper chooses a Student of the Week from both the junior high and high school and runs a photo and a short bio on page two. Doesn't everybody like having their picture in the paper? Students who make the honor roll are listed every quarter, and photos of sports events are plastered across the sports section. There's even a column spotlighting clubs, carwashes, and fund-raisers. It's fun to be a kid in a small town!

Your kids need to adapt to changes in their responsibilities as well. If your country man has a ranch or farm, you might want to start out by giving them a few chores (after consulting with your beau). They can spend time with your guy, and he'll get to know them without Mom's interference. There's always work that needs doing, and extra hands are always welcome.

Helping out on the ranch is part of growing up. By the time country kids are five or six, they may gather eggs, feed chickens, or help plant seeds in the garden. By nine or ten they may start milking goats, picking vegetables from the garden, or helping with dinner. By their teens country kids are raising and showing their own animals or even training for equestrian events. How about the rodeo? Yes, they still have a rodeo queen and rodeo princesses, and they're all expert horsewomen. Country teens may have their own garden (and make pocket money selling produce at the Saturday market), learn to drive the tractor or how to make quilts, including making batts from your own wool.

Imagine everything your kids can see and do! They'll have the benefit of a "real world" education, in addition to formal schooling. They can watch lambs being born, cowboys rounding up cattle, learn to ride and train horses or dogs, be part of construction, agriculture, and forestry—you name it! A farm or ranch is like having a classroom in your own backyard, only you'll have an outdoor laboratory to rival *any* textbook. The icing on the cake is that this outdoor laboratory isn't like "school" at all—it's more like fun!

What if your man isn't a rancher? What if he's a lawyer, businessman, woodsman, or carpenter? He'll probably still have plenty of land for a garden and a few horses, sheep (in the country you don't mow what animals can eat), goats, chickens, and, of course, dogs. Your children will still have the benefits of living on a large ranch, only on a smaller scale.

- If he lives in town, your kids will have easier access to some activities, like after-school programs.

Our country school is the place to be, whether it's athletic competition, the spring concert, or the Christmas pageant. With only two hundred students, K–12th grade, classes are small and everyone knows everyone. If a kid wants to play basketball, there's a place on the team. If your teen is full of pep, she (or he) can be a cheerleader. Your kids will get extra attention and a first-rate education.

It's possible that your children may dress differently from the kids at their new country school. In this environment they'll get on track quicker if they blend in. That may entail some of the shopping I've been advising against, but in this case, fitting in is important.

Your kids are probably in for a bigger culture shock than you are, because you've most likely lived more places than they have. Customs and behaviors will probably be much different from what they're used to. They're bound to feel insecure, and that sometimes results in an "attitude." If your teenage son acquires a big chip on his shoulder, or your little girl demands to move back "home," cut them a little slack.

The tension will lessen as soon as they get a new friend or two. Friends play a key role in whether people are happy, and this may be a tough issue for your children. They'll miss their city friends and will probably want to invite them to the country on weekends.

In this case, I'd suggest you consider limiting those visits, because what they need to do is make friends with country kids.

Don't cut out visits entirely, because you'll only create unnecessary animosity, but do try to spread them out. If your kids spend all their time with city friends, it will only make it more difficult to make new ones.

Hanging on to the past won't help them (or you) build a new life in the country. It's hard to let go of your comfort zone (remember Linus and his blanket?), but at some point both you and your children have to take the plunge. One way to do that is to put a positive spin on this issue. Your children and you, too, can reinvent yourselves! If your son wants to lose his "nerd" image, this is his chance. No one in the country knew that about him anyway. If your daughter was bored with school last year, she has a complete change of scene to look forward to. I spent my youth as an "air force brat," and that meant moving every two years or so. I still remember creating new personas for myself until I settled into my *real* self. Whether it was a change of hairstyle or attitude, moving gave me an opportunity to change things, or at least to try.

If your children insist on sticking to their old ways, there isn't much you can do except to keep encouraging them. If they've never gone out for sports, urge them to give it a try. The competition isn't nearly as tough here as it was in those big schools. If they like to write, suggest they join the newspaper or yearbook staff. If they've made mistakes in the past, remind them that no one knows. If they've got a reputation, they don't have to live up to it.

This move is about change, and that includes helping your children make the best of a great opportunity. With your enthusiasm—and a large dose of patience—they'll soon learn to enjoy their new life in the country.

CHAPTER 32

Doctor, Lawyer, and Indian Chief

One of your biggest adjustments to Country Ways has to do with work. In the city, what you *do* says a lot about who you *are.* To some degree, city people use their job or profession as a way of describing themselves. "What do you do?" and "Where do you work?" are questions frequently heard in the city.

Your response to those questions creates a kind of "composite snapshot" of who and what you are and are not. Whether you're a lawyer, secretary, waitress, doctor, hairstylist, or bookkeeper, each of those words creates an impression about your income, social status, and intelligence. Those impressions aren't necessarily correct, but they do make it easier to label people, and that's more a city attitude than country.

We don't use Instamatic cameras in the country. We

just don't fit into boxes quite as easily as city people, and one reason for that is the way we perceive *work.* In the country we're more focused on making a *life* than a living, so we try to figure out how to derive an income from things that interest us. Sure, some people work a "regular" job, but that doesn't necessarily create that convenient snapshot we've been talking about.

In the country you have to find new ways of getting a handle on "who" a person is. That takes some getting used to, both in how you perceive people and in understanding that country folk don't have an easy way of labeling you, either. You're no longer the "doctor, lawyer, or Indian chief." You're a composite of many things, and it's up to you to communicate those "things" to other people. The assumptions you're used to making, and having made about you, just aren't the same.

I think you might be surprised just how disconcerting this "loss of identity" may make you feel. I remember all too well my own reaction; I went around explaining myself to people—in city terms. I made a point of telling them about my city job, that I'd been an administrator for a *big* (translation: important) law firm, that I had my own office and secretary (translation: important). I hung on to that snapshot as if it were a life preserver. It was my *identity.*

Giving it up was tough, but that's because I didn't have a handle on exactly *who* I was. I sure thought I did, but that journey of discovery didn't start until I moved to the country. That's when I finally had time to ask myself some hard questions and to find the answers. In the city, my job, home, commute, writing, and just *living* left little time for reflection or growth. Creating a new snapshot, one that will reflect your new life, isn't a simple matter. It's important that this new picture encompass a lot more of the *real* you. If it's a *true* picture, you won't be able to develop it right away. Give yourself some time.

My friend Norma works part-time as a cook, but that doesn't tell you much about her. She and her husband, Gene, live on a nice forty-acre parcel about ten miles from town. They breed Jack Russell terriers and registered Corriedale sheep. Norma sells her fleeces, yarn, and hand-knit socks and hats under the trade name "Nelson's Sheep Shed." She's also a founding member of our local fiber arts group and gave me my first spinning lesson. If you ask Norma what she "does," she'll probably tell you about her sheep, dogs, garden, or interest in fiber arts. I knew her for over a year before she mentioned her cooking skills or that she used to be a schoolteacher!

Another friend, Robin, has a family operation. Two generations of her family own 320 acres of prime real estate managed as a multilevel farm. The main house and several outbuildings are only a few hundred yards from the highway, so they have good public access. They raise horses and sheep, give riding lessons, and run a summer camp for children. Robin has a fiber arts studio stocked with exotic fiber, yarn, and knitting and weaving supplies. Every summer the family puts on a week-long spinning and knitting retreat called "Fibervisions." The accommodations include a bunkhouse, enticing meals, wonderful instructors, trail rides at sunset, and great fun!

There are lots of possibilities for making a country living. You only have to find what suits you. How about cashing in on the renewed interest in country life? After all, isn't that what brought you here in the first place? If you have a ranch, develop a half dozen day-long events like buckaroo branding, western cattle roundup, sheep shearing, trail rides, or horse breaking and training. Include a barbecue and storytelling around the campfire. Two very different markets for "ranch days" are families and corporate executives. Business retreats focusing on team building is a new and very lucrative market.

For vacationers yearning to take a journey down the "past lane," spending a few days on a farm would be a slice of heaven. Borrow the idea of "farm stays" from Australia and New Zealand and create your own bed-and-breakfast. If you're not enthusiastic about renting out a spare bedroom, consider remodeling an existing barn or outbuilding or starting from scratch—build a couple of small cabins, complete with front porches, rocking chairs, and pastoral views!

Estate auctions are great places to find old housewares, furnishings, and occasional oddities (like the "Rosebud" sled I bought for $3) that qualify as antiques. A little spit and polish goes a long way toward refurbishing them for resale. I've always thought "antiquing" would be a great way to make a living. There's also a growing interest in handcrafted products such as basket making, woodworking, handmade paper embossed with wild grasses and flowers, soap and candle making, or holiday wreaths.

If you're handy with a camera, how about giving nature photography a try? You could specialize in barns, homesteads, sunsets, forests, wildflowers, wildlife, or farm animals. Advertising agencies and magazines are always looking for photographs for their stock libraries. You could even finish off your photo with a rough-hewn picture frame and move into retail markets.

Another possibility is running a small business from your home. Choose something you enjoy, already know how to do, or can readily learn. Do your homework and plunge right in! Entrepreneurs are alive and well in the country, but they usually just call themselves "self-employed." It does make good sense to *not* put all your eggs in one basket. Instead have two or three irons in the fire!

Take a close look at your city job and see how you can use it to your advantage. Teaching what you already know is an excellent option. Whether you hold classes in your living room or barn or go directly to the customers, put those credentials to work and make friends while you're at it. One of the first things I did when I moved to the country was hang out my shingle as a paralegal. I had years of experience, and after consulting a local attorney for state requirements, I opened for business. Since I live up in the mountains, I traveled to my clients' homes for consultations, then did the work at home. I think this transition helped somewhat with that identity issue I described earlier.

Within a year I was off doing other things and no longer needed a life preserver to get me through the rough waters of transition. Admittedly that took some time, a new perspective, and a lot of help from my country man. But armed with the knowledge you now possess, your adjustment from city to country should be smooth sailing.

CHAPTER 33

Noah's Ark

Another one of those transitions you're going to have to make has to do with animals. If you think I've talked a lot about animals in this book, you're probably right. Whether it's wild animals, herds, flocks, or one old sheep dog, country living and animals seem to go hand in hand. A lot of country men love and care for animals. A lot more own and raise them. If you've never been comfortable around animals, you should at least be willing to have an open mind. Ideally you need to work on changing your perspective to that of an animal lover.

Isn't this one of those things you should look on as a learning experience? After all, you're up for a challenge, or you wouldn't be interested in moving to the country! I'm not saying you have to learn to ride a horse or feed the stock, but if animals are a big part of your man's life, you *do* have to figure out a way to cope. You might find it helpful to remember that country animals are *professionals.* That means they have both a place *and* a purpose—somebody has to keep strangers, coyotes, and mice out of the house or barn. Aren't you glad it isn't you?

Our Great Pyrenees sheepdog, Savannah, is a perfect example of a professional animal. She bonded with the flock when she was a pup, and they're her companions. Sure, she enjoys taking a walk with me in the woods and having her ears scratched, but she doesn't come inside. As for sheep, goats, and domesticated animals you might breed or train, they're a source of income, not pets. If, on the other hand, your guy thinks farm animals belong on the porch, that's a horse of a different color. You have to decide if this is something you can live with or not.

If you don't love animals, it may be because you lump them all together. Yet an interesting thing about animals is that they all have distinct personalities that seem to match their special niche on the farm. Did you know llamas make terrific guard animals? That goats are curious, intelligent, and enjoy hanging out with people? That most dogs are loyal, both to flock and man? That they'll protect your children as well as the herd? Are you starting to change your mind—just a little?

Another tip: Look at the animal kingdom with a touch of humor!

Remember the story about bumper sheep in chapter 27? Did you laugh? If not, go back and read it again. I find amusement and delight in animals, along with the work *and* the profit. Yes, there's profit in animals, whether they're furry or feathery creatures—horses, cattle, sheep, goats, chickens, angora rabbits, or more exotic animals like peacocks and llamas. Some are big, others small, some expensive, some not. There's something to suit everyone, even if it's just one ornery hound dog.

Some animals that city people think are cute are looked at quite differently in the country. Take squirrels—please take the squirrels! We refer to those little pests as "tree rats." They steal eggs, and that's a hanging offense in the country. Last summer I watched four chickens gang up on a thieving squirrel. He'd grabbed an egg and was contemplating lunch when four chickens surrounded him. The next thing I knew, that little squirrel was being pecked and tossed in the air. Each hen took a turn because they probably weren't sure which nest he'd raided. The chickens killed the squirrel, and I didn't blame them one bit.

Don't forget the business of raising show animals (horses, dogs, llamas, and many other possibilities—even chickens and rabbits) for fun and profit. If that's where your interest lies, you may be following the show circuit three months out of the year. That can be expensive, but it can also be exciting, profitable, and a lot of fun.

If you have children, animals can be a big help in their transition to the country.

Most kids yearn for a dog (at the least), and taking care of animals is a good way for kids to learn responsibility. If your children become part of 4-H, raising a lamb is the next step, followed by the county fair, competition, and blue ribbons. This is a great thing for your kids and you, too!

The early days of spring bring both wildflowers and babies. (Okay, they come at other times, too, but I'm taking a little poetic license to get a point across.) Cuddly lambs, spunky kids (baby goats, not children!), bawling calves, and long-legged colts are both cute and delightful. They lift your spirits and give you a sense of purpose for the coming season. That's all good. But the bad news is learning you can't keep them *all.* Country living will bring many new ideas into your life. One of them is nature, and I don't mean Disney film nature.

The reality of living on a farm or ranch is that animals are bought and sold, live and die. That's a difficult adjustment if you've never been around animals—other than the zoo, nature parks, or movies. If you have children, this may be a hard dose of reality, but given a little time, they *will* adjust. Living with the cycles of nature will give your children a new awareness of themselves in relation to the natural world around them. Life is a series of lessons, and important ones go along with the discovery that every creature has a place and purpose and that the renewal of life goes on.

In time, you'll feel as though the animals on your place belong there as much as you do. Their bloodlines will span generations, just as in your own family. You'll get to know the animals on your ranch or farm, and they'll contribute a lot to your life. And if your man loves white-faced sheep and all you see is wet wool, remember, this is the country. With so many animals to choose from, you're bound to find one or two you can love!

CHAPTER 34

Partners for Life

Country men and women feel the same about relationships. They expect their share of stormy weather and a crisis or two along the way. But they don't run, and they don't hide. They face their problems head on, and they face them together. The slow, measured path is the road *most* traveled in the country because there's a mountain of riches along the way. No waiting around for a silly rainbow to find a pot of gold. It's there for the taking every day. A good life, family, friends, and someone special by your side.

Country Ways means you're in this life together, a partnership of two that's stronger than either of you alone. When you feel a bond with nature and the land, long-term is a way of life. Remember, "You don't own the land, the land owns you." Once you've been in the country for a while, you'll understand the truth to that country saying.

If you've gone over to the country side of life, *forever* is what your man has in mind.

No heading down the road when times are tough, no splitting up, no divorce. Let a country man know you can go the distance, and you'll capture his heart. Remember, he doesn't see an end, only the beginning and the rest of his life. You should feel that way, too.

Country men and women spend a lot of time together. In most cases their relationship is a combination of best friends, lovers, parents, and business partners. Those roles aren't compartmentalized. You can't pull one rabbit out of the hat and leave a few more hidden inside. There's no magic trick or wave of a wand. It's just plain, hard work. You're not looking at being *just* his wife or significant other; throw in partner in life, love, and business, and stir like crazy. Sound like a lot? It is!

I don't want to scare you off. If you're more comfortable leaning on him than playing a starring role, that's okay. He needs someone to comfort and nurture, too. Having you fill that important niche will make him stronger. Your love and support can mean the difference between failure and success. When you're ready to tackle projects of your own, he'll support you all the way. In fact, he'll bust his buttons (or snap his suspenders) over your success. There's nothing a country man likes better than bragging about the woman he loves.

Living in the country creates intimate bonds that just aren't possible in the city. You'll see your guy in every role life brings him, from farmer to financial planner, on top of the world one day to "I'm too bone tired to move" the next. A country man isn't a "one-trick pony." He's a generalist, not a specialist. He knows how to fix things and how to make do with what he has. He's resourceful and knows a little about everything. If he doesn't, he'll track down what he needs like a bloodhound. You can depend on him—and should. It'll please him to help you with anything, anything at all.

You can work side by side or separately, but when you come together at the end of the day, you'll have plenty to talk about, dreams to share, successes to cheer, and an occasional loss to mourn. This move from city to country will take some getting used to, and you'll have to be patient. He can help with that. After all, he's waited a lifetime for you. What's a few months or a year?

Remember, the *slow, measured path* leads to success. That applies to your relationship, too.

Don't expect everything to be smooth as silk. There's sure to be some bumps and hard knocks along the way. And remember, what sometimes seems like the most difficult of times can also be the best. I had one of those "life-changing" experiences during my second summer in the country. With our summer also comes the "fire season," and my dreams of country life never included standing alongside neighbors on a fire line, fighting to save my home. Although it was something I'll never forget, the experience also gave me something I'll always cherish—a sense of belonging. I paid my dues. This place is *mine!*

I don't know what rites of passage you will experience in the country. I don't know what problems you and your man will overcome together or what it is that will bring you closer. I only know that bonds are created not just when times are good, but sometimes when they're particularly difficult. When you travel down a rough road together, and still manage to arrive at your destination together, that's something to celebrate. My life experiences and *emotions* are the things that gave me a sense of place, a feeling of ownership and belonging. It's a feeling that goes clear through to the bone. It's something no one could have explained to me and that no one can ever take away.

Just hang in there. Your destination is in sight, but you've got to allow for a few soft shoulders on the learning curve. By the way, it may be a little late to mention it, but this is probably going to be the most difficult relationship of your life. That's because a country romance is very different from what you're used to, and so is the man. The ground rules have changed, and so has your life. You're also taking a new look at how your job, work, or career relates to your life. These issues aren't for the faint of heart.

Your country relationship is also going to be the *best* you've ever had. Aren't good things worth waiting and working for? You betcha! You've started down the dangerous, winding road that took me from life in the fast lane to love in the "past" lane. It was tough at times, but I wouldn't trade a minute of the last seven years. I envy your beginning and just wish I could look over your shoulder. The best I can do is offer some advice. The best you can do is take it.

Your country man will bring out qualities you've been hiding under a bushel basket all your life.

If you're shy, he'll chalk it up to being sweet as springtime. If you're outgoing, he'll enjoy your exuberance. He'll appreciate your intelligence or simplicity, your skills or desire to learn. Your hard work and dedication will make him love you all the more. Country folk are industrious. They don't draw a big line between work and everything else. They take great pride in accomplishment. He'll tell you when you're doing a great job. Do the same for him. After all, if work is what you do every day, why not enjoy it?

Partnerships, whether in love, life, or business, are difficult. When you roll them all into one big package, things are bound to go awry once in a while. When that happens, keep sight of what's waiting for you at the end of the line—everything you've ever dreamed of. It's worth all the time and energy you've already invested and will *still* invest. You never stop working at life *or* love, if you really want the best!

CHAPTER 35

The Payoff

If you've read this whole book, you're definitely serious about Country Ways. I'm impressed! I know I haven't made the journey sound easy, because it isn't. I just hope I haven't made it sound too difficult. Finding my country man and my new home have brought me "the good life," and I'd like to invite you to be my neighbor. In case you're still asking yourself if the rewards are worth the changes we've been talking about, here's an all-too-brief reminder of what's in it for you.

1. A man who wants to be both your best friend *and* lover. A confidant who'll stand proudly by your side or watch from a distance, and be comfortable doing either. A partner who'll share your beliefs in time-honored values like trust, honesty, and mutual respect.

Someone who will appreciate all the things you do and, what's more, say so!

2. A relationship that will bring out the best in both you and your man. Love will shine through your life and bring you a sense of peace, security, and well-being. It's wonderful to be in love and to give that love back. You'll find a renewed sense of purpose and desire to build a strong foundation for this new life together.

3. A stronger *you.* The country way of life will give you strength, both in mind and in body. Having a partner you believe in, and who believes in you, will enhance your sense of self. You can (and will) climb any mountain!

4. A slower, healthier pace of life that runs in neutral and even a comfortable idle at times. An opportunity to slow down and create the scenery of your life, rather than watching it speeding by with no way to stop the train and get off. A chance to breathe fresh air and live a less stressful, more centered life.

5. The opportunity to rethink your career goals and to focus on work that will enhance your life. Think about this idea of "making a life instead of a living." Once you understand the power in this concept, you'll understand why retirement is only for people who don't enjoy what they do for most of the day.

6. A place where family and community are important, where people know the meaning of friendship and will offer to help when you need a hand. You'll feel the same way about them! A place where you can be part of something and make a difference in your own corner of the world.

7. A safe place to raise your children. A place where they can learn life's lessons without making a fatal mistake and get on with discovering who they are and want to be. A place with a lower crime rate and as far from gangs as you can get.

8. An opportunity to gain a new perspective that *more* is not necessarily *better.* A place where the simple things in life *do* matter and *can* make you happy. Understanding that you have the power to determine the quality of your own life instead of having it thrust upon you.

9. Time to be thankful for the bounties of the human spirit, to get in touch with, and understand, what touches your heart.

10. Most important of all, you'll find a place to call home, and a man to love, that you'll never want to leave.

CHAPTER 36

Happily Ever After with Country Ways

With the land and family as your main focus, you and your country man have the foundation for a lifetime together. You may be a family of two, or you may have children. Your family may or may not include relatives, but it will surely include people who share your vision of country life and Country Ways. You'll build lifelong friendships, and your children will grow up together. You're planting seeds now, but with hard work and a lot of love you'll reap the rewards the rest of your life.

Sit on the back porch and look at the wheat fields stretched out like a high, golden carpet for half a mile. Watch cattle the color of tawny brown, coffee, and russet grazing in the pasture, with calves at their side. Listen to the sound of crickets after dark and dogs barking in the distance. The soft rustle of spreading oaks that shade the back of the house in summer. The sound of snow falling in winter.

Enjoy the seasons of the earth and of your love. Spring brings the joy of falling in love, summer the hard work of sustaining life, autumn the time to harvest, and winter the period for rest. Be generous with your love, especially in the first few years. Those days and nights will form a relationship that will last the rest of your life, see you through the tough times, and bring a smile when you think back to the beginning of this country life together.

Don't miss opportunities to build memories with your man. Years from now you'll laugh about the time you hauled calves to auction and got *two* flat tires. You'll remember quiet conversations at dawn, tender moments at dusk, sleepy sighs at midnight. Watching him head out into a blinding rainstorm when the sheep broke through the fence. Helping bring foals into the world. The many times you walked country lanes together or hiked for miles along a seasonal creek. Cuddling up close on the old porch swing on cool autumn nights.

Remember the little things that mattered so much in the beginning. Take the simple things to heart and keep them close always—how you met, the first time he held your hand, and how you went about building a life together. See the good in each other and all the discoveries along the way. Travel the back roads together and experience the beauty of the natural world.

You aren't missing anything by being away from the

bright lights of the city. The more complex your life, the more problems you have. By rushing everywhere, we often don't get anywhere worth going. In the country you learn how to make a life instead of a living. You're experiencing how things were meant to be. The good things. The true worth of a man, love, companionship, and the land.

You are a pioneer traveling in new territory. Expect to take a wrong turn occasionally or to lose your way. Your man will help you along the road. He may feel lost at times, too. That's when it's your turn to take his hand. Make this life a journey of discovery. Consider all you have to look forward to.

If you think this is too much work, that you could never make it in the country, I've got a suggestion. Go back to page one and start over. Give it another try. There's a chance you may still understand. This *is* a better way to live. Country Ways *are* worth waiting and working for. Good luck, and may you find all the happiness you deserve on the country road ahead.